PEOPLE FIRST.
SAFETY ALWAYS.

REBUILDING CULTURE FROM THE INSIDE OUT

MICKEY HANNUM

To my beloved parents, who taught me to chase my dreams and find joy in my journey. You believed in me even when I faltered, instilling in me the courage to persevere. Though my deepest regret is not completing this book during your lifetime, your unwavering faith in my abilities continues to inspire and guide me every day. This book is for you, with all my love and gratitude.

CONTENTS

INTRODUCTION:
EMBRACING A NEW ERA OF SAFETY LEADERSHIP

As a leader, manager, supervisor, or safety professional, imagine walking into a workplace where safety isn't just a rule—it's a culture ingrained in every decision, conversation, and action. What if "Safety First" was more than a mantra, becoming instead a dynamic mindset driving transformational leadership and cultivating empowered teams? Welcome to "People First. Safety Always: Rebuilding Culture from the Inside Out," where the journey to redefine safety begins precisely at its core—people.

This book heralds a paradigm shift, illustrating how safety transcends compliance to become a foundational pillar of operational excellence and human value. It challenges traditional perspectives, encouraging leaders at every level to foster an environment where safety is a continuous, people-driven journey. Through meticulously researched insights and real-world examples, "People First. Safety Always" provides practical strategies to embed safety into the corporate consciousness, ensuring it becomes an intrinsic part of everyday operations.

Whether you're responsible for a single team or an entire organization, the role you play is pivotal. Transforming safety into a shared principle is not just about implementing new procedures—it's about igniting passion and accountability in every individual. Leaders will discover methods to engage teams authentically, nurturing environments where each member feels both responsible and empowered to maintain the highest standards of safety. This book is a journey of empowerment, offering tools for you to lead with purpose, ensure alignment with core values, and inspire transformative change across all levels of your organization.

"People First. Safety Always" is your guide to navigating the complexities of modern safety beliefs. It is a call to action for leaders everywhere to transcend traditional safety practices and reimagine what is possible when people are placed at the heart of safety initiatives. Join us as we embark on this transformative journey to rebuild culture from the inside out, one empowered leader at a time.

CHAPTER 1:
FOUNDATION OF
COMPLIANCE

"A chain is only as strong as its weakest link."
- Thomas Reid

In the realm of safety, compliance is the sturdy foundation upon which excellence is built. It isn't the end goal—it's the launchpad. Before we innovate or aspire to safety excellence, we must root ourselves in clearly defined policies, standards, and responsibilities. Only when this base is strong can we reach higher. This book opens with a focus on compliance because it is essential—we need well-defined standards, norms, procedures, policies, and programs as our bedrock. Only then can we confidently explore and transcend to the realms of safety excellence.

Compliance is more than adherence to rules. It signals our commitment to the communities we operate within and stands as a testament to our integrity and responsibility. This foundation is not just an obligatory measure; it is the framework that supports and guides innovation and improvement in safety practices.

As you engage with this book, you'll realize that recognizing the value of compliance as the starting point does not restrain us; rather, it equips us with the tools necessary to dream bigger, reach higher, and achieve best practices that truly go beyond compliance. Let's embark on this journey, starting with the essentials before we capture the extraordinary.

Imagine stepping into a manufacturing company where meticulous compliance is crucial. In this environment, every detail matters—from updating safety protocols to ensuring each employee understands and adheres to regulations. The famous "Safety First" motto is prominently displayed everywhere. By meeting these challenges, the company safeguards its operations and earns its rightful place within the community, affirming that maintaining compliance isn't solely an obligation; it's a strategic cornerstone.

Step into the bustling safety office—employees return inspection forms, check out PPE, and ask questions about training. At the center of it all is Linda, clipboard in hand, fielding queries with calm authority. She's more than a compliance officer; she's the compass guiding daily operations through regulatory waters.

Imagine this scenario: one day, an email alert surfaces about a potential regulatory change that could impact the company. Linda springs into action, rallying her team to dissect the implications, update protocols, and organize a workshop to disseminate this critical information to every employee. This isn't just a box-ticking exercise; it's Linda orchestrating a compliance symphony where each note ensures harmony with the law. Having people like Linda is instrumental in achieving and maintaining compliance.

Just as Linda embodies the spirit of compliance, organizations need structured systems that reflect and support their proactive approach. Enter the management system—a framework that scales Linda's vigilance into an organization-wide commitment.

Compliance is not just a barrier against legal troubles; it is the foundation upon which safety excellence is built. Without a strong compliance framework, aspirations toward superior safety measures lack the solid ground to be effectively realized. Compliance is your true permit to operate, anchoring your company legally and morally within the community while uniting teams under a banner of shared values and safety commitments. Compliance is often seen as the mundane part of business operations, but it is so much more.

Let's explore what it means to construct a robust compliance program, dive into the significance of an effective management system, and examine how leadership sets the tone for compliance across the organization. Stay tuned as we dig into these critical elements that set the stage for not just compliance, but elevated safety leadership.

To effectively embed compliance beyond an obligation, a well-structured compliance program is vital. This program acts as the blueprint for seamlessly integrating rules into daily operations, requiring comprehensive training, transparent policies, and regular audits. Such proactive programs anticipate and address potential risks, shielding organizations from legal issues while fostering trust, efficiency, and innovation. For enhanced compliance efforts, incorporating a comprehensive management system is key. This system, akin to the architecture of a skyscraper, strengthens the compliance framework. It uses systematic processes for risk identification, training, monitoring, and evaluation. A meticulous management system ensures consistency, providing a centralized point of reference to align organizational goals, minimizing errors, and enhance accountability across all levels.

First and foremost, implementing a meticulous management system ensures consistency and uniformity across the board. It's about having a centralized point of reference that aligns all parts of an organization with the same compliance goals, reducing errors, and discrepancies that might arrive form inconsistencies. This, in turn enhances understanding and accountability at every level – from frontline employee to the executive suite.

Secondly, these systems are designed to evolve with the ever-changing compliance landscape. New regulations can appear on the radar with little warning, adding layers of complexity to existing protocols. A dynamic management system is agile, capable of adapting to such changes seamlessly. This agility not only ensures ongoing compliance but also positions the organization as proactive rather than reactive.

Furthermore, adopting a robust management system underscores the importance of leadership involvement. When leaders endorse and actively participate in these systems, they send a powerful example, emphasizing that compliance isn't just a task—it's a fundamental component of the organization's values. Leaders become champions of compliance, fostering a workplace where staying compliant is regarded not as an obligation, but as a shared, honorable pursuit. They inspire their teams to adhere to high standards, thereby elevating the entire organization's approach to compliance.

By establishing and nurturing such a system, organizations set themselves up for continual improvement. Each compliance activity tracked, each training program completed, feeds back into the system to be assessed and refined. This creates a loop of perpetual betterment, where lessons learned fuel future enhancements, ensuring the compliance program not only survives but thrives amidst growing demands and expectations.

Implementing a robust management system within an organization is a critical step towards ensuring comprehensive compliance and fostering a mindset of continuous improvement.

However, it is not just a matter of installing software or drafting policies—it requires a strategic plan that aligns with organizational goals and incorporates scalable technology solutions.

Crafting a strategic plan is vital, as it serves as the roadmap guiding the implementation of the management system. This plan should start with a thorough assessment of the existing compliance landscape, identifying strengths to build upon and gaps that need bridging. Engaging stakeholders from various levels within the organization is also crucial during the planning phase to gather insights and buy-in, ensuring that the system is tailored to real-world challenges and gains universal support.

A well-conceived strategic plan outlines clear objectives, timelines, responsibilities, and resource allocations, providing a structured pathway to implementing the system efficiently. It emphasizes the dynamic nature of compliance and underscores the need for the system to be adaptable to legislative changes and organizational growth.

The landscape of Environmental, Health, and Safety (EHS) software offers numerous solutions designed to streamline compliance efforts. With a wealth of options available, choosing the right software becomes a strategic decision in itself. EHS software packages can automate routine compliance tasks such as monitoring incidents, tracking regulatory updates, and managing documentation. This not only reduces human error but also frees up resources for strategic initiatives.

Many of these software solutions offer customizable dashboards, real-time data analytics, and automated alerts, promoting a proactive approach to compliance. The integration of EHS tools into a management system ensures that compliance becomes an integral part of everyday operations rather than a series of ad-hoc tasks.

For instance, a mid-sized chemical company used EHS software to automate training renewals and regulatory reporting. Within a year, compliance discrepancies dropped by 30%, and managers reported more time to focus on innovation and safety leadership.

Beyond technology, leadership plays a crucial role in implementing an effective management system. Leaders must champion compliance initiatives, modeling adherence to standards and reinforcing the importance of compliance through clear communication and resource allocation. Their visible commitment to the management system signals its significance to the rest of the organization, embedding compliance into the corporate culture.

Continuous improvement is driven by regular evaluations of system performance and stakeholder feedback, allowing the organization to refine processes and update strategies as necessary. The ultimate goal is to create a robust, adaptable compliance ecosystem that not only meets but exceeds regulatory requirements, paving the way for safety excellence and operational integrity.

By strategically implementing a management system that leverages the latest EHS software and promotes leadership involvement, organizations position themselves for compliance success as well as long-term growth and sustainability.

A well-implemented management system establishes a strong compliance culture, aligning every department under a unified strategy and fostering continuous improvement and leadership engagement. This integration is vital for transforming compliance from an isolated checkbox requirement into a dynamic component of organizational success.

Building a robust compliance program through an effective management system is akin to laying a solid foundation for a grand architectural masterpiece. This groundwork unifies every department under a cohesive strategy, creating a seamless pathway for continuous improvement and engaging leadership. However, compliance alone does not guarantee safety excellence. Think of compliance as your ticket to the game—the required entry that enables you to effectively navigate the safety landscape. Organizations can identify unprotected gaps and unexplored areas when they strive to be beyond compliance.

Now, imagine having your systems perfectly aligned with every regulation, yet the reality of injuries still looms. This is where we shift from simply checking boxes to transforming our approach to safety. It's about moving from passive adherence to active engagement, embracing what truly makes a workplace exceptional in safety standards.

In our next discussion, we'll dispel the misconception that equates compliance with safety. By challenging the status quo, we will explore strategies that genuinely elevate our safety practices. It's not just about compliance; it's about embedding a value that anticipates, prevents, and cares. Stay tuned as we transform the way you think about safety and compliance; the adventure is just beginning.

Let's address a common misconception: *the belief that 100% compliance equals 100% safety.* Regulations are intended to, nor can they prevent every injury in real life scenarios. They are not written in a way to address every type of hazard or scenario an employee may encounter. In reality, you could be sitting in an office, confidently asserting that every system aligns perfectly with current regulations while still facing severe workplace injuries. How is that possible? Having every "i" dotted and every "t" crossed in compliance doesn't necessarily shield your workplace from accidents— it simply signifies that you're meeting legal obligations. While compliance is necessary, it is not sufficient in itself to create safety excellence.

Relying solely on these basic requirements means organizations miss out on opportunities to explore innovative safety practices that genuinely prioritize and adapt to the unique dynamics of their work environments.

Having a compliance system in place is like owning a high-quality car equipped with safety belts and airbags—it fundamentally protects you. However, achieving true safety excellence, that coveted zero-harm environment, resembles a proactive driver who avoids risks before they arise. It involves nurturing a culture that actively identifies potential hazards, innovates in workplace safety practices, and continuously improves.

Compliance is critical and non-negotiable—it's your permission to operate and a baseline promise to your stakeholders for a safe, legal workplace. For genuine safety excellence, organizations must scrutinize how injuries can occur in their environment. It's about dynamic leadership, fostering proactive safety initiatives, and integrating innovative practices that prioritize people over procedures. It's in this stride beyond the baseline where real safety transformation occurs.

As we conclude this chapter, remember compliance isn't the ceiling—it's the ground beneath our feet. From here, we must dream bigger, lead stronger, and build workplaces where safety isn't just a rule, but a culture.

In the next chapter, we'll challenge the boundaries of compliance and ask—what does it take to move from only meeting standards to redefining them? What does it take to go beyond compliance? Let's step into the future of safety leadership.

CHAPTER 2:
A PAINFUL REMINDER

"The wise man learns from mistake of others."
– Harry Myers

Why Safety is My Passion... There are moments in life that shake us to our core, and for me, that day came on a bright, seemingly normal afternoon. It was like any other until my phone rang. It was a call that no one plans for—a voice on the other end bearing unimaginable news: a workplace accident had claimed the life of a dear friend.

This was not just any friend; he was vibrant, full of life, and deeply dedicated to his work. His tragic passing resulted not from random misfortune but from a cascade of avoidable lapses, hidden in the shadows of a system that prided itself on being "compliant." Even while every measure was in place on paper, the reality of his absence underscored a harsh truth: compliance alone is insufficient. It can foster a false sense of security, allowing preventable failures to slip through the cracks.

This heartbreaking loss ignited something within me, transforming passive compliance into a fervent mission for active responsibility. It serves as a stark reminder of why I chose safety as my life's work—so no family, no friend ever has to hear or deliver such a call.

Tragedy struck close to home again when I lost a beloved family member to a workplace incident—a moment that forever changed my perspective on safety and responsibility.

Not long after, another family member faced the unbearable loss of his brother-in-law, who was more than family—he was his best friend. These weren't just accidents; they were turning points.

This mission runs deeper than duty for me—it's personal. It's the fire that drives me to make a difference, to ensure that no one else experiences the pain we've felt. This is more than a cause; it's a deeply personal pledge to honor those we have lost and to protect those still with us.

I wake up every day committed to this cause, driven by the unwavering belief that everyone deserves to return home to their loved ones. Because what we do—or fail to do—isn't just about systems, policies, or regulations; it's about people, their safety, and their lives. This mission is not just professional—it's deeply personal, a commitment I uphold to honor those we've unnecessarily lost and to protect those still with us.

Having shared how deeply personal and passionate I am about ensuring everyone gets home safely, it's clear that our daily professional lives extend beyond mere tasks—it's about caring for people. This is why focusing solely on compliance is never enough. While rules and checks lay the groundwork, they often mask the core issues that become heartbreakingly apparent only when tragedy strikes.

My story, sadly, isn't unique. Across industries, similar tragedies unfold—proof that these issues transcend any single workplace or moment. One such example that gripped national attention was the Upper Big Branch Mine disaster in West Virginia.

In the lush landscapes of West Virginia, a significant episode unfolded, echoing the crucial lesson that commitment to safety must exceed regulatory compliance. This next section examines the events of the Upper Big Branch Mine disaster, providing a stark illustration of why we must relentlessly pursue proactive safety leadership to prevent such occurrences. Let's explore how we can transcend compliance to create genuine models of safety excellence.

On April 5, 2010, nestled in the beautiful rolling hills of rural West Virginia, a quiet catastrophe was brewing beneath the surface. The Upper Big Branch Mine, an expansive coal mine operated by Massey Energy, became the scene of a horrific explosion—the deadliest U.S. mining accident in four decades—that claimed the lives of 29 miners. This disaster resulted from a lethal combination of methane gas buildup and coal dust explosion; a grim sequence exacerbated by a series of preventable safety oversight failures.

Investigators determined that the catastrophe was not a random act of fate. It was, to a large extent, a predictable and preventable failure rooted in a culture that prioritized production over people. Massey Energy, a prominent player in the coal mining industry, had been repeatedly cited for safety violations, yet the company's response to these warnings epitomized a compliance-centered approach rather than a people-first, safety-always mindset.

The mine faced hundreds of safety violations leading up to the disaster, including failures in proper ventilation, inadequate dust control, and faulty equipment maintenance—all critical oversights. Instead of addressing these issues, Massey Energy often treated them as inconveniences, fostering a pervasive culture of legalism that prioritized minimum compliance over a commitment to safety excellence. This legalistic attitude created an environment ripe for disaster, imparting a painful lesson to the industry that still resonates today.

The aftermath of the disaster illuminated the necessity of cultivating trust and accountability over superficial compliance. The outrage stemmed not only from the loss of life but also from the underlying culture of neglect. Families and survivors demanded more than surface level accountability; they sought truth, transparency, and transformation in the industry's safety performance. A movement emerged, advocating for reforms that prioritized protective measures and significant investments in safety, pushing for a paradigm shift from simple rule-following to building organizational trust and responsibility.

In the wake of the disaster, there was a significant push to review and reinvigorate the requirements of the Mine Safety and Health Act introduced in 1977, aimed at strengthening safety laws. However, the law's true impact extended beyond its text; it served as a catalyst for redefining safety leadership, urging organizations to focus on creating workplaces where employees felt empowered to speak up without fear of retribution.

The Upper Big Branch tragedy revealed that real change originates from leadership that genuinely values safety over profits. Responsible leaders must cultivate environments where safety is a core principle integrated into daily operations and decision-making. They need to inspire a shared vision, ensuring that every team member feels empowered to uphold safety protocols that protect their lives.

This story serves as a stark reminder that striving for compliance without genuine commitment can lead to catastrophic consequences. The disaster underscored blindly checking boxes is meaningless without the courage to prioritize people over production. Elevating safety beliefs requires trust, transparency, and transformational leadership. Real breakthroughs occur when organizations move beyond a checklist mentality and embed a people-first, safety-always belief at every level.

As we continue to explore the necessity of transcending compliance in safety, let's draw inspiration from these profound lessons. Let them guide us toward a future where everyone, from the boardroom to the production floor, embraces accountability and builds a robust culture of trust that prioritizes the well-being of all.

Compliance without care often creates a false sense of security. As we have seen, this mindset can cost lives and carries a financial burden that organizations cannot afford to ignore. The financial implications of workplace injuries are starkly felt across various industries. Companies, in their quest to maintain operations and assure employees' safety, frequently encounter significant financial burdens when accidents occur. These costs include immediate medical expenses, long-term rehabilitation, and compensation for lost wages, along with indirect costs such as legal fees and increased insurance premiums.

What does a single workplace injury truly cost a business? The National Safety Council estimates the average cost at $1,100 per incident, a number that multiplies quickly when indirect costs are considered. According to the NSC, workplace injuries cost U.S. businesses a staggering $171 billion annually, encompassing wage and productivity losses, medical expenses, administrative costs, and employer liabilities. This statistic underscores the urgent need for businesses to pivot from compliance to cultivating an environment that yields transformative economic and ethical outcomes.

The Occupational Safety and Health Administration (OSHA) further details that direct workers' compensation costs reach nearly $1 billion per week. These figures illustrate the tangible financial strain companies endure. Beyond direct costs lie hidden expenses that accumulate over time, such as training replacement workers, lost productivity, and damage to customer relations and corporate reputation.

These financial realities vividly demonstrate that companies investing early in safety protocols can avoid debilitating expenses. For example, analysis by the Liberty Mutual Workplace Safety Index suggests that for every dollar spent on improving workplace safety, companies can expect a $4 return due to reduced injuries and associated costs. Safety leadership transcends regulatory requirements; it involves developing a proactive strategy that integrates safety into the organizational values. This integration not only results in financial savings but also enhances employee morale, engagement, and productivity. A culture rooted in trust, rather than relying solely on meeting regulatory requirements, significantly reduces workplace injuries and alleviates the economic impacts on businesses. By emphasizing trust and employee engagement in safety practices, companies create environments where workers are more likely to adhere to safety procedures, report hazards, and contribute to improvements in workplace safety protocols. This collaborative approach reduces compensation costs and fosters a more cohesive and resilient work environment.

The cornerstone of effective safety practice is cultivating a safety mindset that permeates the workplace. An ownership mentality in safety means that every individual, from the shop floor to the executive suite, actively participates in the dialogue about safety measures and their continuous improvement. This mentality encourages initiative—prompting employees to identify, report, and rectify potential hazards without waiting for directives from higher-ups. Leaders are responsible for creating an environment where everyone feels comfortable voicing concerns and suggestions.

For instance, consider the transformation at Alcoa under CEO Paul O'Neill, who redefined the company's values by elevating safety above profitability and productivity. O'Neill's bold move—making safety the number one agenda item at every meeting—sent a powerful message. He wasn't just protecting workers; he was building trust across the organization. Through his unwavering commitment, safety evolved from a compliance checklist to a deeply ingrained core value. This shift not only enhanced O'Neill's credibility within the organization but also catalyzed a significant reduction in workplace injuries. As a result, both employee morale and productivity soared while profitability and stock prices increased, proving that when safety becomes a central value, it can transform a company's overall performance.

An ownership mentality thrives in an environment of empowerment and trust, where employees feel secure enough to voice concerns and suggest improvements without fear of reprisal or indifference. This requires more than policy changes; it necessitates cultivating a mindset where safety is a shared responsibility and a collective success.

Leaders set the tone for an organization's culture, and their commitment to safety directly influences the practices and attitudes of the workforce. Effective safety leadership goes beyond issuing safety protocol edicts; it involves modeling the behaviors that leaders deem important and championing safety as an unequivocal principle. Leadership in safety is exemplified through consistent, visible engagement in safety initiatives, adequate resource allocation to safety measures, rewarding both proactive and corrective actions taken by employees, and fostering honest conversations.

Organizations like Alcoa demonstrate how leadership serves as a critical driver of cultural change. Under O'Neill's leadership, safety discussions became central to meetings, with employees encouraged to innovate solutions to potential hazards, thereby integrating safety deeply into the company culture. By demonstrating their commitment to employee welfare, leaders like O'Neill ignite motivation and reinforce the idea that every worker has a stake in maintaining a safe work environment.

Using safety as a central driving force to enhance organizational values is crucial because it creates a foundation of trust and reliability, as exemplified by Alcoa's success. Prioritizing safety fosters an environment where employees feel valued and protected, leading to increased morale and engagement. This commitment to safety transcends into meticulous attention to detail, which improves operational efficiencies and quality. It encourages proactive identification and mitigation of potential issues, contributing to continuous improvement. Furthermore, a strong safety mindset boosts an organization's reputation, attracting talent and strengthening customer and stakeholder confidence. When safety is paramount, it not only prevents accidents but also drives excellence across the board, ensuring sustainable growth and success.

Many companies remain entrenched in a compliance mindset out of inertia, unaware of the transformative potential of a team-driven culture. However, some organizations have successfully redefined safety practices. One notable example is a Midwest manufacturing firm that, upon recognizing the disconnect between safety practices and employee engagement, shifted to an empowered safety model. This transformation was catalyzed by open forums where employees could voice safety concerns that management actively addressed, demonstrating genuine commitment. Leaders asked probing questions about the work and actively listened to the responses.

As a result, the organization experienced a significant drop in workplace incidents, alongside enhanced employee satisfaction and morale. The accountability and respect fostered through this cultural shift not only prevented accidents but also cultivated a more collaborative and engaged workforce—clearly illustrating that cultural transformation in safety extends beyond physical safety to emotional and psychological well-being.

When I reflect on my friend's tragic accident, I often find myself asking, *How could this happen?* He had a young child and his whole life ahead of him. That loss hit me hard and ignited my desire to understand safety better. I knew I had to take action.

But here's the truth: safety professionals can't shoulder this responsibility alone. We need committed leaders who are willing to step up and drive meaningful, lasting change. Creating a culture of shared responsibility in safety doesn't occur by chance; it requires intention, commitment, and, most importantly, heart.

The Pike River Mine disaster in New Zealand on November 19, 2010, became a pivotal moment, underscoring the urgent need for a shift in safety practices. Despite compliance with existing safety regulations, 29 lives were tragically lost due to an explosion. This catastrophe highlighted deep-rooted issues of complacency and a lack of genuine accountability towards worker safety, emphasizing that only aiming to meet compliance is insufficient. Investigations revealed failures in hazard management and ventilation, driven by values that prioritized productivity over safety. Even with legal compliance, lives were lost—reminding us that a true culture of care must be established long before the law requires it.

In response, New Zealand implemented significant reforms in health and safety regulations, but the real transformation stemmed from a societal shift towards prioritizing workplace safety as a fundamental cultural value. The Pike River incident serves as a cautionary tale for various industries, illustrating the profound human cost of neglecting safety. Genuine accountability for safety must be deeply embedded within the organization, empowering individuals at every level to embrace it as a core priority. As we transition to exploring personal impacts on safety performance, the importance of individual commitment to drive change is underscored, advancing from compliance to a culture of trust and responsibility.

In the next chapter, we'll spotlight individuals who are changing culture from the inside out—because this mission isn't just about systems; it's about people taking action.

Ask yourself, "What actions have I been taking as a leader to transform culture?" before moving on to the *Heart of Safety – People*.

CHAPTER 3:
THE HEART OF SAFETY – PEOPLE

"Leading well is not about enriching yourself-it's about empowering others."
– John C. Maxwell

BP's Deepwater Horizon disaster in 2010 triggered a significant safety transformation within the company. In response to the crisis, BP introduced the "My Safety, Our Safety" initiative, shifting the focus from compliance to fostering personal accountability in safety practices. This program encouraged employee engagement at all levels, aiming to create a sense of ownership and community responsibility for safety outcomes.

The cornerstone of this initiative was the active engagement and empowerment of employees to leverage discretionary energy—going beyond job requirements to emotionally invest in the company's safety goals. Through workshops and open forums, employees were given a platform to share concerns and ideas, while safety champions were established in departments to lead by example, reinforcing a supportive environment for safety innovation.

The results were profound, evidenced by a 60% reduction in safety-related incidents and a 200% increase in proactive safety suggestions over three years. Employee morale and productivity also improved, showcasing the broader organizational benefits of deeply engaged employees. This initiative not only transformed BP's safety metrics but also set a benchmark for safety leadership across the industry alongside Shell Oil.

In the realm of industrial safety, transitioning from solely meeting standards to fostering a culture of trust can significantly enhance operational safety outcomes. Shell Oil's Hearts and Minds safety program offers a compelling case study in how safety leadership can achieve transformative results.

The Hearts and Minds program emerged from the need to address deep-rooted safety challenges within Shell Oil, a global leader in energy production operating under potentially hazardous conditions. Established in the early 2000s, the program was designed to empower employees and cultivate an environment of proactive safety engagement. This initiative became crucial after a series of incidents that highlighted existing safety inefficiencies, sparking a drive for cultural change.

The core philosophy behind Hearts and Minds is to engage employees at all levels in viewing safety not merely as rules to obey but as a personal and collective responsibility. While compliance with safety regulations is essential, true safety excellence arises from each individual's belief in its importance and commitment to safe practices.

To achieve this cultural shift, Shell employed several strategic measures within the Hearts and Minds framework. The program involved interactive workshops and sessions encouraging employees to share their experiences, fears, and suggestions regarding workplace safety. These sessions were designed to break down barriers, allowing open communication and learning among employees at all levels.

A notable aspect of the program is its emphasis on behavioral science principles. Shell recognized that changing safety behavior required motivating internal reflection among employees rather than simply issuing directives. The program incorporated tools such as the "Risk Assessment Matrix," helping workers visualize potential hazards and their consequences, urging them to adopt safer practices.

Empowerment was another significant component. By fostering a climate where employees felt they had a say in safety procedures, Shell encouraged a sense of responsibility and accountability. Leaders within the organization were trained to embody and promote the values of Hearts and Minds, shifting from a directive role to one of support and coaching.

The transformation did not occur overnight. Initial resistance was met with persistence, as Shell understood that building trust and changing habits require consistent effort and reinforcement. Regular safety audits, feedback loops, and incentive programs motivated adherence to safe practices by rewarding teams that demonstrated significant improvements.

The impact of the Hearts and Minds safety program was profound. Over time, Shell reported a substantial decrease in injury rates and a notable improvement in safety attitudes among employees. The program's success is evident in the reduction of Lost Time Injury Frequency (LTIF) rates and a more engaged workforce committed to safety.

In addition to quantifiable gains, one of the most important achievements of the program has been a paradigm shift within Shell's values. The Hearts and Minds initiative has shown that when employees trust their leadership and feel empowered to prioritize safety, the entire organization benefits through enhanced operational efficiency and reduced accidents.

The Hearts and Minds program has since been recognized and adopted by various organizations worldwide as a model for safety leadership. It exemplifies how cultural transformation driven by trust and engagement can lead to sustainable safety improvements, aligning perfectly with the book's thesis that moving beyond compliance can yield transformative results.

Shell Oil's implementation of the "Hearts and Minds" program, initiated in the early 2000s, serves as a powerful example of the benefits of transitioning from a compliance-focused culture to one based on trust and personal accountability. Prior to the program, Shell recorded approximately 17 injuries per million working hours; after embracing this approach, injury rates decreased significantly to fewer than 4 per million working hours. Key to the program's success were leadership commitment, employee engagement, and a focus on emotional and cultural change, resulting in increased reporting of near misses and proactive safety interventions.

These examples from BP and Shell affirm what we intuitively know: when people are trusted, included, and empowered, they become the driving force behind meaningful safety change.

Policies don't create safety—people do. The moment you shift from enforcing rules to empowering individuals, everything begins to change. You stop chasing compliance and start building commitment. Real ownership doesn't stem from more checklists or tighter controls—it emerges when people believe that safety isn't just their responsibility; it's their voice and their choice.

Gallup's landmark study found that engaged workplaces experience 70% fewer safety incidents. This reflects a broader organizational trend where engagement fosters proactive safety initatives. Engaged employees are more mindful and adhere better to safety protocols, significantly reducing the risk of accidents.

The benefits don't stop there; engaged teams also report lower healthcare use. For instance, the Journal of Occupational and Environmental Medicine documented a 32% reduction in medical visits. Moreover, companies investing in safety report high returns; one analysis showed businesses saving $4 for every dollar spent on safety improvements.

The message is clear: engagement isn't a nice-to-have—it's a strategic imperative with tangible, organization-wide returns.

Crucial to fostering engagement is leadership. Leaders who emphasize the importance of safety inspire a shared sense of responsibility among employees. A shipping company experienced a 50% reduction in lost-time injuries after adopting a participatory leadership style that engaged staff regularly and involved them in safety decisions. Engaged employees not only comply with safety procedures; they embody a culture where safety thrives as a collective value.

When people feel trusted, they act with care. They speak up—not out of obligation, but because they know their voices matter. When they become part of the solution, they invest in the outcome, transforming simple tasks into meaningful contributions. Safety excellence isn't just a system or slogan; it's a collective movement driven by individuals who choose to care, lead, and look out for others.

If you aim for a safer, stronger culture, start with trust and build with ownership. Your people are the breakthrough you've been seeking—a community where giving their best becomes intrinsic, not obligatory. Cultivating this environment ensures that everyone is inspired to excel beyond compliance.

Picture a warehouse worker who notices a loose cable lying dangerously in the path of an active forklift. Instead of walking by, assuming someone else will handle it, she pauses to secure it, eliminating the hazard, and promptly informs her supervisor. This act of discretionary energy—though not in her job description—is driven by care and a sense of responsibility.

That's the power of discretionary energy—the extra effort employees choose to give when they're truly engaged. It all begins with trust. When trust is present, a ripple effect occurs: people feel empowered, take the initiative, and own their work in ways that exceed basic job descriptions.

Trust is the root, the starting point of every great workplace relationship. When employees know they're trusted—not just managed—they step up. They go the extra mile because they want to, not because they are told to.

Empowerment fuels autonomy. Trust-based relationships provide employees with the space to make decisions and share their ideas. This freedom drives motivation and sparks real ownership.

Engagement follows connection. When people feel seen, heard, and valued, they connect deeply with the mission. This sense of belonging inspires them to contribute discretionary energy where it matters most— whether driving innovation, solving problems, or ensuring safety.

Toyota's approach to workplace safety exemplifies the power of discretionary energy and empowerment. Embracing the jidoka principle, Toyota allows workers to halt production the moment a problem is detected. This isn't just about stopping a line; it's a powerful display of trust, granting employees the authority to act decisively.

The andon system reinforces this trust, turning every worker into a guardian of safety. When an issue arises, workers can pull an andon cord, immediately prioritizing safety. This approach fosters an environment where employees proactively step up, feeling genuine ownership and responsibility.

This system is a cultural shift towards engagement and empowerment. When employees are entrusted with responsibility, it activates their discretionary energy, leading to higher commitment and a safer work environment. The effectiveness of this approach was clearly demonstrated during the 2010 recalls, where Toyota reinforced these systems, showcasing their integral role in maintaining product integrity and workplace safety.

Some say there's no silver bullet in safety. I say there is—and *it's your* people. When we stop managing safety at people and start building it with them, we transform workplaces forever. When you stop throwing safety at them and start building it with them, everything changes. Engagement rises, risks decrease, and safety becomes something they own, not something they must comply with.

CHAPTER 4:
BUILDING TRUST

"The best way to find out if you can trust somebody is to trust them."
– Ernest Hemingway

In the bustling corridors of a leading manufacturing corporation, where machinery hummed alongside human activity, seeds of mistrust between employees and management had taken root. The company had endured a series of safety incidents, each chipping away at employees' confidence in their leadership. Although safety protocols were meticulously outlined in manuals and drilled into staff, they remained largely ineffective. Compliance was achieved, yet accidents persisted, leaving a pervasive sense of insecurity. Enter Michael Daniels, a relatively new manager with a successful track record in transforming workplace safety. Under his leadership, a profound transformation was about to unfold—an evolution from compliance to trust.

Michael's approach to safety was unconventional, moving away from the authoritarian compliance checks that characterized his predecessors' efforts. On his first day, he gathered the entire staff to address the elephant in the room—the lack of trust. In a candid conversation, he acknowledged past mistakes, framing them as a collective responsibility. "Mistakes have been made," he admitted openly. "But these mistakes will not define us. Trust me; we will transform this place together."

The pivotal moment came when Michael equipped himself not with a clipboard of checklists but with a commitment to listening. He spent weeks meeting with teams, understanding their challenges, and learning from their stories. He asked pointed questions: "What makes you feel unsafe? What would make you feel safer? Where do you think the next accident might occur? How severe will it be? What controls do we have to prevent it?" The answers revealed a common thread—that policies, no matter how stringent, were lifeless without mutual respect and openness.

To materialize this insight, Michael pioneered a "Safety Trust Initiative," a departure from traditional compliance-centric models. This initiative was unique; its foundation was dialogue and shared responsibility. Employees became agents of change, encouraged to develop their own safety protocols that resonated with their everyday experiences and needs. Here, empowerment flourished—employees transformed from obedient followers to proactive stakeholders in safety.

Courageous steps followed. A safety committee was formed, comprised entirely of volunteers from various departments, placing the power of safety oversight in the hands of those entrenched in daily operations. These committee members acted as safety beacons, their credibility stemming not from hierarchical authority, but from a genuine commitment to their colleagues' well-being.

The results were remarkable. Within months, the company recorded a dramatic decline in safety incidents. The numbers were driven not by enforced compliance but by organic team efforts fueled by shared values and trust. Michael's relentless pursuit of trust through empathy and accountability fostered an environment where employees felt seen and heard, transforming the company entirely.

"The true measure of leadership is not how much we accomplish, but how much we empower others to achieve." Michael's words resonated at a final all-hands meeting celebrating their accomplishments. His leadership style was not about dictating rules but about building bridges of trust that empowered each employee to take ownership of safety—bridges that would later prove foundational to maintaining a culture of trust and safety long after his departure.

The transformation journey led by Michael Daniels exemplifies how trust-driven leadership is essential for cultivating a healthy and safe work environment, where compliance becomes a byproduct of genuine engagement and shared responsibility rather than an enforced obligation. His story serves as a guiding light for those in leadership positions aiming to foster environments where every individual feels compelled and inspired to prioritize not only their own safety but also the safety of their colleagues.

Trust is not built overnight. It requires consistent effort and authenticity. As leaders, we should strive to create environments where trust is the norm. This foundation enhances safety and drives innovation and collaboration. By embodying trust in our leadership, we can inspire profound change and create lasting impact in our organizations.

Michael Daniels didn't just improve compliance—he transformed the workplace. His game-changing leadership turned safety from a rulebook into a shared mission, proving that empowered people are the most powerful safety strategy of all. How can we apply these principles to our own teams and workplaces?

To build trust within your team, start by fostering open communication—invite concerns, welcome ideas, and listen without judgment. Lead by example, consistently displaying honesty and reliability in all interactions.

Empower employees by giving them real ownership of safety practices, along with the tools and autonomy to implement their ideas. Treat mistakes as an opportunity to learn rather than failures to penalize. Finally, celebrate contributions, recognizing effort as it fuels the trust you're working to build. This integrated approach ensures that trust becomes the foundation of an engaged and committed team.

While Michael's story illustrates trust-building at a team level, global organizations like DuPont demonstrate how these principles can be scaled to transform entire corporate cultures. This shows how trust, as a leadership linchpin, can ripple through an organization, fostering environments where safety is both a value and a practice embraced by all.

In the ever-evolving landscape of organizational safety, the shift from compliance driven initiatives to genuine trust has proven transformative. This chapter explores the role of trust in safety leadership, highlighting how nurturing this critical element can significantly reduce workplace incidents. A poignant case study exemplifying this shift is DuPont, a global science and innovation company that, through deliberate trust-building initiatives, significantly enhanced its culture and outcomes.

DuPont, known for its rigorous safety standards, faced a pivotal moment in the early 2000s. Despite having compliance-driven safety protocols, the company experienced several incidents that revealed a crucial gap: the need for trust-based safety leadership. Recognizing that compliance alone was insufficient, DuPont embarked on a transformative journey to integrate trust into the fabric of its culture.

The company's strategy revolved around three pillars: communication, empowerment, and accountability. Through town hall meetings and anonymous feedback, they cultivated a transparent environment where employees felt safe to voice concerns and suggestions without fear of reprisal. This openness was essential for building an atmosphere where everyone felt their voice mattered—a core aspect of trust.

Empowerment was equally vital, as employees were given authority to halt production if they identified safety hazards. This demonstrated the company's deep trust in its workers' judgment, fostering a profound sense of ownership and responsibility for maintaining a safe workplace.

Simultaneously, accountability was strengthened through regular audits and peer reviews, ensuring a balanced environment where empowerment was supported by responsibility. This blend of trust and accountability fostered a shared mission for safety, transforming it from a rulebook requirement into a company-wide commitment.

The results of DuPont's trust-based approach were significant. Within three years, the company reported a 20% reduction in workplace incidents. This was not simply a consequence of enhanced safety protocols but reflected the newfound culture where employees were united in their commitment to safety.

The trust-driven model encouraged a proactive rather than reactive approach to safety. Employees felt a personal responsibility for their own safety as well as that of their colleagues, leading to innovative solutions emerging from within the workforce.

Beyond reducing incidents, the confidence-rooted environment at DuPont fostered a mindset of continuous improvement. Safety metrics became a collective responsibility, celebrated and scrutinized in equal measure. Employees began to see themselves as integral to the safety narrative, maintaining momentum for engagement and improvement.

DuPont's experience highlights the substantial impact trust can have in redefining safety leadership. Trust was not just a complement to compliance but a catalyst, transforming safety from a mandated policy into a shared value.

We've previously touched on Alcoa, but to fully appreciate the transformative power of trust, it's worth examining Paul O'Neill's revolutionary leadership. Alcoa exemplifies how trust in safety leadership can lead to impactful outcomes. When O'Neill became CEO in 1987, Alcoa faced significant safety challenges that affected morale and efficiency. His pioneering focus on safety as a core value emphasized trust, laying the groundwork for remarkable improvements. Through this exploration, we'll uncover how Alcoa's strategic shift underscores the broader relevance of trust across various organizational dimensions.

The Approach: Safety as a Daily Agenda

O'Neill's strategy was revolutionary—he made safety the central focus of every meeting and conversation across the company. He believed that improving safety outcomes required more than compliance; it demanded trust.

- **Daily Safety Meetings:** Each shift began with safety meetings where teams discussed potential hazards and preventive actions. These gatherings encouraged open dialogue, allowing employees to feel their safety concerns were heard and valued. They were genuine conversations, not just check-the-box meetings driven by a mantra of "Safety First."
- **Open Channels for Reporting:** Alcoa ensured that all employees had direct lines of communication to leadership for reporting safety issues without fear of repercussions. This transparency built trust across all organizational levels.
- **Unified Focus on Safety:** O'Neill positioned safety as a metric for organizational excellence, asserting that an incident-free

workplace reflected a well-managed company. This unified focus created a shared vision that brought employees together.

The results were striking. Within a year, Alcoa's lost workday injury rate drastically decreased. Over a decade, the company reduced its rate from approximately 1.86 lost workdays per 100 workers to virtually zero.

The strong emphasis on safety as a performance priority fostered a workplace where trust was integral. Employees felt confident in their roles, knowing that their well-being was the company's top priority. This trustful environment also led to improved productivity and innovation, as employees were more engaged and willing to contribute ideas without fear of pushback.

O'Neill's leadership style was instrumental in transforming Alcoa's culture. By prioritizing safety and instilling trust, he not only improved the physical safety of the workplace but also enhanced cooperation and a sense of community among employees.

Alcoa's experience highlights how trust-based safety leadership yields both quantitative and qualitative benefits. By embedding safety as a fundamental organizational value, Alcoa not only enhanced trust and performance but also realized significant overall business benefits. Prioritizing safety led to improved operational efficiencies and product quality, directly impacting the bottom line. Financially, this paradigm shift reduced costs associated with accidents and legal issues, while boosting productivity and innovation. Ultimately, robust safety mindset contributes to higher employee morale and engagement, fostering an environment conducive to sustained competitive advantage across all facets of the business.

When examining the actions of Michael Daniels, the leaders at DuPont, and Paul O'Neill at Alcoa, a powerful pattern emerges—rooted not in top-down mandates, but in a deep, intentional commitment to trust. These leaders didn't start with spreadsheets or safety manuals; they began with people. They walked the floors, asked questions, listened deeply, and made it clear: safety wasn't a program; it was a promise and a mindset. Daniels built psychological safety into everyday conversations, DuPont empowered people while strengthening accountability, and O'Neill made safety his non-negotiable principle, signaling to every employee that their well-being mattered more than profits—and ironically, or perhaps predictably, profits soared.

These stories impart a simple yet profound lesson: when leaders choose trust, safety becomes a shared mission—not a mandate. With trust, engagement grows. Innovation flourishes. Performance follows. Thus, the question isn't what system you'll launch, but what trust-building action you'll take. Real transformation begins not with a new rule, but with a human choice.

CHAPTER 5:
PSYCHOLOGICAL SAFETY

"Trust leads to approachability and open communications"
-Scott Weiss

In the noise of modern industrial workplaces, where machinery hums and tools clang against metal, one element often stands as the silent guardian of safety: psychological safety. This chapter explores an intriguing example of how a team achieved remarkable safety results by fostering an environment where openness and communication were the keys to unlocking exceptional performance.

The story begins in a bustling manufacturing plant on the outskirts of Des Moines, Iowa. Known for its innovative designs and high-pressure environment, the plant operated under an unspoken rule of silence that discouraged workers from voicing concerns for fear of reprisal or ridicule.

Driven by her commitment to transformative leadership, plant manager Lisa Martin recognized the need for change. Inspired by Amy Edmondson's "The Fearless Organization," which emphasizes the importance of psychological safety in fostering open communication and innovation, Lisa set out to reshape the culture of her factory.

She gathered employees for a series of workshops addressing the elephant in the room—emotional security. Lisa introduced the concept with passion, explaining that true safety extended beyond just following procedures; it required ensuring that everyone felt secure enough to speak up. She encouraged workers to share their experiences, suggestions, and concerns openly.

To foster this environment, Lisa implemented key changes. She introduced regular "safety huddles," where teams gathered informally to discuss safety issues, share stories, and collaborate on solutions. These huddles operated under a simple rule: every opinion was valid, and every voice deserved to be heard.

Initially, some employees were hesitant, conditioned by years of silence. However, Lisa's commitment to open communication soon began to yield results. One employee, Mike, who oversaw quality control, timidly shared a routine issue he had hesitated to mention for months—certain machinery was prone to minor but frequent malfunctions that could lead to larger problems if left unaddressed. Instead of dismissing Mike's concerns, the team acknowledged the issue and collaborated on a strategy to address and mitigate potential issues.

The openness fostered by emotional security among team members led to more than just improved communication. Employees began taking ownership of their responsibilities, suggesting improvements, and actively participating in developing safety protocols. Lisa's trust in her team empowered them to propose innovative solutions, resulting in a significant drop in workplace incidents and a boost in overall morale.

The results were staggering. Over the following months, the plant recorded a 30% reduction in accidents and near misses. Employees reported increased satisfaction, reflected in lower turnover rates and enhanced teamwork. The belief in openness transformed the plant from a place of quiet compliance to one of vibrant collaboration.

Lisa's example is not just inspiring; it is instructive. It illustrates what emotional security looks like in action and emphasizes why it is more than just a metric for performance. Her story invites us to ask: what creates that sense of safety, and how can we as leaders cultivate it across our teams and organizations? Transitioning into a broader perspective on psychological safety, her leadership highlights its critical role, paving the way for deeper exploration into how these principles can be embedded at every level of leadership.

Edmondson's research allows teams to transition from compliance-driven environments to those embracing trust. By enabling employees to voice concerns and contribute to decision-making processes, organizations can enhance safety outcomes while driving innovation and resilience.

This narrative serves as an introduction to the broader theme of the chapter: the realization that creating an environment of openness forms the backbone of a culture that transcends compliance, nurturing a workplace where individuals are not just workers but partners in progress.

Psychological safety is not just a buzzword; it is an essential leadership quality. For supervisors guiding teams daily, it means cultivating an environment where people feel heard, valued, and unafraid to speak up. This kind of culture doesn't just happen; it is modeled, nurtured, and profoundly felt, becoming the bedrock of team cohesion and innovation.

A culture rooted in confidence is the invisible thread that holds high-performing, trusting teams together. It embodies the belief that individuals won't be punished or humiliated for speaking up with ideas, questions, concerns, or even mistakes. When people feel safe, they stop bracing for judgment and start leaning into creativity, vulnerability, and real collaboration. It is the space where innovation flourishes, and trust takes root—not because everyone always agrees, but because everyone knows they can be authentic.

So, as a leader, ask yourself: *Do people feel safe to be fully themselves around me?* Psychological safety is not an accident; it is created through everyday actions. Consider one supervisor I know who starts every meeting by asking, *"What's one challenge you've faced this week—and what did you learn from it?"* That consistent question fostered a culture of honesty and learning over time, allowing team members to express vulnerabilities and insights without fear. This environment is created through your responses when someone challenges a decision, how you provide space for quieter voices, and how you frame missteps—not as liabilities, but as opportunities to grow. Creating such empowering environments leaves a powerful legacy. When people feel genuinely safe, they don't just complete tasks— they bring their full selves to their work. This is where **discretionary energy** comes to life!

It's one thing to say you are empowered and a partner; it's another to live it. The truth is, simply stating the words doesn't create an experience. People don't feel safe just because a leader mentions the concept in a meeting or includes it in a slide deck. They feel safe when they see it and experience it in action—through consistent, everyday behaviors. That's why leaders should focus less on the term psychological safety itself and more on **how their actions invite openness, respect, and trust.**

When employees feel emotionally secure, they don't just comply—they engage. They report hazards early, collaborate openly, and offer ideas to improve safety systems. It is this proactive energy, born of trust, that prevents incidents before they happen.

By emphasizing continuous improvement and employee engagement, psychological safety ensures that potential hazards are promptly noted and rectified. Engaged employees are more vigilant and actively contribute to identifying risks, thus driving a culture of ownership. This leads to improved safety outcomes and a more resilient organization overall.

Bridging these insights with a literary reflection, we turn to Golding's "Lord of the Flies." This classic work illustrates the collapse of order and the rise of fear in the absence of psychological safety. Piggy's voice is silenced, Jack's reign symbolizes toxic leadership, and Simon's fate underscores the loss suffered when fear suffocates trust. Though dramatic, these themes resonate in workplaces where the absence of trust breeds silence and decay, underscoring the need for a foundational culture of confidence and openness.

Creating an atmosphere free from apprehension, where people feel safe to speak up, requires effort and empathy—qualities essential for genuine organizational change and effective safety leadership. By fostering an environment where employees trust that their concerns will be acknowledged and valued, organizations can move beyond compliance to achieve transformative safety results. This understanding is essential for leaders intent on building a future-oriented culture that values human elements at its core.

As we dive deeper into the backbone of safety, let's remember how easily the absence of psychological security can alter the course of an environment, just as it did on Golding's island. Our workplaces are not deserted islands. With deliberate action, we can ensure that fear doesn't dictate the climate and that every voice has a chance to be heard, thereby fostering a truly safe and thriving workplace.

Culture doesn't stem from slogans—it is built in the quiet, consistent moments when leaders listen deeply, respond with respect, and make it safe to speak the truth. These moments whisper, *"You matter."* When every voice is honored, safety evolves from rule to principle. This transformative action starts with a choice—a choice that every leader can make. It's the foundational step to cultivating an engaged, proactive team where discretionary energy thrives. Remember, real change is deeply personal; it emerges from those small but powerful actions that leaders take daily.

CHAPTER 6:
LEARNING FROM EVENTS

"The only real mistake is the one from which we learn nothing."
– Henry Ford

In the early 2000s, a major chemical manufacturing company faced a critical situation that would forever change its approach to safety. This case stands as a testament to the transformative power of learning from incidents rather than succumbing to a culture of blame.

The company, ChemicalCo (a pseudonym to preserve anonymity), was known for its adherence to standard safety protocols. However, beneath the surface of compliance, the leadership failed to recognize the potential of a deeper, more transformative approach to safety management.

In the fall of 2002, an incident occurred that would serve as a catalyst for change. When Mark suffered burns during a routine procedure, he braced for the worst. Like others before him, he expected blame. However, something different happened—and that shift would change everything.

Instead of pointing fingers, the company chose to look deeper—at the processes, the systems, and the culture itself. They focused not on punishing Mark but on learning how to ensure it never happened to anyone else.

Real accountability isn't about blaming one person; it's about everyone owning safety together. That's how excellence is built: not through fear, but through a shared commitment to improvement.

The operational leader at ChemicalCo recognized that blame cultures are detrimental because they often focus on punishment rather than understanding and resolving underlying issues. Leadership knew that continuing to blame individuals would lead to misinformation, lack of trust, and an environment where employees are afraid to report problems or suggest improvements.

Recognizing the need for a more effective approach, ChemicalCo adopted Root Cause Analysis (RCA) to shift focus from blame to understanding systems. Despite this, many safety leaders questioned whether the corrective actions were truly impactful. This pondering led to a pivotal realization: the insights from those doing the work were crucial, spurring deeper inquiry into frontline feedback and marking a game-changing moment that reshaped their safety strategy.

They had spent years relying on written procedures—neatly organized, carefully documented, yet somewhat disconnected from reality. Then, someone asked a simple question: What if we just talked to the people doing the work? Not just about what should happen, but about what actually happens.

A technician insightfully remarked, "The manual tells us what to do—but we know how to do it safely." This insight reshaped leadership's perspective on procedural design.

So, they did. They began having meaningful conversations—curious, open-ended discussions with the operators, technicians, and engineers who lived the process every day. This sparked a realization that procedures alone weren't sufficient.

These conversations revealed not only what was working but also how teams succeeded despite the procedures. They shared creative workarounds, near-misses, and instinctive practices that kept people safe but had never been documented.

The spark came during their Process Hazard Analysis (PHA) meetings— cross-functional gatherings required by OSHA's process safety management standards. These meetings transformed from completing regulatory driven checkboxes into opportunities for leaders, managers, engineers, supervisors, and operators to learn from one another in unprecedented ways. Someone finally asked, "Why stop here?"

Why not apply the same approach—not just to prevent explosions, fires, or equipment failures—but to uncover the small cracks in our system that lead to injuries? And why not ask the most important experts—the workers themselves—how they manage to stay safe while getting the job done?

This marked a shift from top-down instruction to collaborative discovery. From assuming to asking. It changed everything. Through these methods, ChemicalCo discovered that Mark's accident was not solely due to operator error but a combination of ambiguous procedural instructions, inadequate training on specific equipment, and other daily challenges. This revelation led to significant improvements in their training programs and operational procedures.

As ChemicalCo transitioned from blame to learning, the impact was tangible. The company fostered an environment where employees felt safe discussing failures and near-misses. This cultural shift encouraged proactive identification of potential hazards, substantially reducing the rate of accidents.

ChemicalCo became a learning organization—one that embraces continuous improvement and views mistakes as opportunities for growth rather than threats. By focusing on learning, the company not only improved safety but also enhanced employee morale and engagement. Workers felt valued and understood their role in the larger safety ecosystem.

This approach drew inspiration from other successful learning organizations. Notably, the airline industry, renowned for its safety record, emphasizes learning from incidents through non-punitive reporting systems and comprehensive analysis frameworks. Their model demonstrates that prioritizing systemic understanding over individual blame can yield significant safety improvements.

ChemicalCo's transformation echoed a broader principle known as *Operational Learning*, which values real-time insight over rigid control. This approach is vividly illustrated in one of history's most high-stakes problem-solving stories: Apollo 13. Here, the blending of frontline insights and collaborative problem-solving showcased how addressing complexities directly can lead to innovative solutions.

In "Apollo 13," after an oxygen tank exploded on the spacecraft, Gene Kranz and his team relied on collaboration rather than manuals. Faced with an unprecedented crisis, they worked across disciplines, dismantling hierarchies and testing solutions in real-time. Their success stemmed not from compliance but from trust, experimentation, and learning—qualities that define Operational Learning today. This mirrors the shift experienced at ChemicalCo, illustrating that effective safety excellence arises from shared insights and real-time problem-solving.

When Mark, a young operator, suffered chemical burns on the job, he braced himself for the worst, fearing blame or discipline. But something different happened.

Instead of pointing fingers, the company chose to look deeper—at the process, systems, and culture itself. They focused not on punishing Mark but on learning how to prevent similar incidents in the future.

Real accountability isn't about blaming one person—it's about everyone owning safety together. That's how excellence is built: not through fear, but through a shared commitment to improvement.

When we stop pointing fingers and start asking better questions, we unlock the true engine of safety: shared accountability, learning in action, and the courage to change. That's how excellence is built—not through fear, but through curiosity and care.

As a leader, it's crucial to pause and reflect: What does shared accountability genuinely look like in my organization? Am I fostering an environment that drives shared ownership, where every team member feels accountable and engaged? The answers to these questions are pivotal. Remember, shared accountability isn't just a concept—it's reflected in daily interactions and the culture we cultivate. So, ask yourself: does your workplace empower everyone to contribute and feel valued?

CHAPTER 7:
SHARED OWNERSHIP

*"The leader builds dispersed and diverse leadership –
distributing leadership to the outermost edges of the circle to
unleash the power of shared responsibility"*
– Frances Hesselbein

Let me take you to the bustling floor of Wilmo Manufacturing, where the constant hum of machines harmonizes with the buzz of industrious workers. Among them is Mike Reynolds, an assembly line worker known for his sharp eye and quick thinking. Mike isn't just any worker; he is a catalyst for change and an opinion leader others admire.

One day, during his lunch break, Mike noticed something concerning: the safety signage, those vital reminders for maintaining a safe workplace, had grown faded and less visible over time. It was a small detail, but Mike understood its potential to contribute to accidents, as people might enter areas without the correct PPE or come into contact with moving equipment. Inspired to act, he proposed a simple initiative: a bi-weekly "Safety Sweep," where employees voluntarily checked and reported on infrastructural issues affecting safety. Mike's supervisor recognized his efforts and encouraged others to join in the process.

What began as a simple idea soon gained traction. Mike's initiative didn't just address worn-out signs; it evolved into a cultural shift, empowering employees to voice safety concerns. More importantly, it blurred the lines between traditional roles, making safety a shared responsibility rather than something managed solely by the safety officer. As more employees embraced this collective approach, the incident rate plummeted, and morale soared, proving that when everyone takes a stake in safety, it transforms from a protocol into a pervasive culture.

This story powerfully illustrates that the journey beyond compliance begins with embracing safety as a shared duty. It's not confined to job titles or isolated in specific departments; it's a collective commitment across every level of the organization. As we delve into this chapter, we will explore how adopting this mindset and encouraging similar initiatives can redefine safety standards in any workplace.

Mike's story reflects a deeper truth: when people feel empowered, safety becomes everyone's business. To truly achieve safety excellence, organizations must move beyond checking boxes. Like Mike, they must embrace safety as everyone's responsibility. When employees at all levels take ownership—speaking up, collaborating, and holding each other accountable—safety transforms from a policy into a way of life.

This breakthrough is paramount for several reasons:

When safety becomes a collective commitment, every employee actively participates in maintaining and improving safety standards. This collective involvement transforms passive compliance into proactive vigilance, motivating workers to identify and mitigate hazards before they escalate. This heightened engagement results in a more attentive workforce, capable of spotting potential issues early and brainstorming actionable solutions swiftly.

Shared responsibility fosters a collaborative environment rich in diverse perspectives and experiences. By breaking down hierarchical barriers, teams can freely exchange ideas and strategies, leading to innovative safety solutions.

For instance, a maintenance worker might suggest alterations to equipment handling protocols that significantly reduce injury risk—insights perhaps less visible to leadership alone. This synergy enhances safety practices and reinforces a culture of respect for contributions at all levels.

In an empowered workforce with shared safety responsibility, accountability extends beyond individual performance to encompass team-based outcomes. When all employees realize that safety failures impact the entire team, they are more inclined to adhere to protocols and encourage their peers to do the same. This collective accountability ensures that safety standards remain top of mind, as everyone is invested in upholding the organization's well-being and success.

By embedding safety into the organization's fabric, resilience against unforeseen challenges is significantly bolstered. An ownership culture equips teams to respond rapidly and effectively to new challenges, adapting protocols dynamically as needs evolve. This adaptability is rooted in trust—trust that each team member is committed to safety, even when facing unexpected challenges. **There will be a true belief in People First – Safety Always!**

Finally, shared responsibility ensures that safety practices are not only effective but sustainable. As individual contributions to safety are recognized and valued, loyalty and morale soar, reducing staff turnover and fostering organizational stability. Moreover, employees who feel empowered to influence safety are more likely to uphold best practices, ensuring that safety strategies endure beyond initial implementation phases. It's about creating an ownership mindset that fuels vigilance, innovation, and long-term success.

What role do supervisors and managers play in creating a shared mission where safety is truly embraced by everyone? I've been asked that question more than a few times throughout my career, and my answer is always the same: they play a crucial role. Leadership sets the tone, especially at the front line. When supervisors and managers lead with ownership, accountability, and care, it inspires everyone around them to do the same. That's how a genuine belief of shared safety ownership is born—from the top, through every layer of the team.

Leadership is pivotal in fostering an organizational mindset of safety ownership. When a leader models a commitment to safety, it sends a powerful signal for the entire organization. Here's how effective leadership can drive ownership and why failing to do so undermines the effort:

Leaders must embody the principles of safety they wish to see mirrored in their teams. This includes demonstrating consistent adherence to safety protocols, proactively identifying risks, and encouraging open communication. When employees observe their leaders prioritizing safety, they recognize its value and are motivated to act similarly. This modeling of behavior is crucial in setting the tone for organization-wide adoption of safety as a shared responsibility.

A leader who fosters an environment of trust and openness encourages employees to voice safety concerns without fear of criticism or retaliation. This psychological safety is foundational for innovation and vigilance in safety practices. Employees are empowered to contribute ideas and report issues proactively, knowing their insights are valued and considered. Leaders must actively listen and respond constructively to safety concerns, ensuring organizational processes support continuous improvement through feedback loops.

When leaders neglect these responsibilities, several issues can arise, and it can happen quickly:

If leaders are seen as disregarding safety or not taking it seriously, it sends a message that safety isn't genuinely valued. This can lead to disengagement and reduced morale among employees, who may feel their safety is secondary. A lack of visible commitment from leadership often results in a culture where safety is viewed as an unwelcome imposition rather than a shared duty.

When leaders do not create an atmosphere that values safety innovation, it hampers employees from proposing creative solutions to improve safety practices. Absent leadership support, many workers might hesitate to speak up, fearing reprimand or ridicule. Consequently, valuable insights from those most familiar with day-to-day risks—such as frontline workers—remain unheard. This stifles the organization's ability to adapt and enhance its safety initiatives.

A failure to model ownership and advocate for safety erodes trust within the organization. Employees need to believe that their leaders genuinely care about their well-being, a belief that must be consistently reinforced by leadership actions. Without trust, any efforts to engage employees in shared responsibility for safety can seem insincere and ultimately ineffective. A supervisor who looks the other way when something isn't quite right creates an unintentional culture detrimental to achieving safe outcomes.

Leaders hold a critical role in promoting a culture of safety ownership by modeling the behaviors they wish to see, fostering psychological safety, and engaging employees in meaningful ways. Failing to embody these principles undermines safety initiatives and alienates employees from participating actively, ultimately stalling progress toward safety excellence.

In the ever-evolving landscape of workplace safety, the transition from solely striving to meet compliance to cultivating a model of trust and shared ownership has emerged as a powerful catalyst for transformation. This shift is vividly exemplified in the case of DuPont, a manufacturing giant that embraced this paradigm shift and witnessed remarkable improvements in its safety performance.

DuPont, renowned for its groundbreaking innovations in the chemical industry, is equally recognized for its pioneering approach to workplace safety. The company's commitment to safeguarding its workforce began to crystallize in the early 20th century when it faced significant challenges due to recurring accidents and safety mishaps. The realization that compliance alone was inadequate prompted DuPont to embark on a transformative journey centered around shared ownership and shared responsibility.

The turning point came when DuPont adopted a safety management system that fostered trust and involvement at all organizational levels. They launched the initiative "Stop, Think, and Act," empowering every employee to take ownership of safety by encouraging proactive measures and immediate action. This approach not only required adherence to safety protocols but also nurtured a climate where each worker felt responsible for their own safety and that of their colleagues. The central idea was that by cultivating an environment of trust, employees would be more invested in safety, leading to reduced incidents and enhanced overall well-being.

DuPont's total recordable incident rate dropped nearly 80%, from 2.1 to 0.4, over a decade—clear proof of what happens when safety becomes a shared value.

This collective ownership of safety extended beyond DuPont's operations as the company began consulting for other businesses, helping them replicate this success across various industries. The principles of shared responsibility were applied in settings ranging from manufacturing to construction, with DuPont leading workshops and training sessions to demonstrate the power of trust-based cultures.

Moreover, DuPont's leadership recognized that effective communication was crucial in maintaining this culture. They introduced regular safety meetings and forums where employees could voice concerns, share experiences, and collaboratively brainstorm solutions. These platforms helped break down hierarchical barriers, reinforcing the idea that every individual, regardless of rank, played a vital role in fostering safety.

The overarching implication of DuPont's case is that organizations characterized by integrity and care lead to sustained improvements in safety outcomes. By embedding shared ownership into the organizational values, DuPont not only reduced accidents but transformed its workforce's mindset about safety, encouraging a culture where safety is viewed as a shared moral responsibility.

Take a moment to reflect—what would happen if every person in your organization truly felt a sense of ownership? How would that change the way people show up each day? Imagine the strength, trust, and momentum a team could build.

Now get ready—because in the next chapter, we'll explore how leaders can turn this vision into reality. We will address one of the most critical pieces of the puzzle: how leaders can engage and inspire a culture where safety isn't just a rule—it's a way of life! **People First – Safety Always!**

CHAPTER 8:
ENGAGING LEADERSHIP

"If your actions inspire others to dream more, learn more, do more, and become more, you are a leader."
– John Quincy Adams

Let's jump into the real-life journeys of two leaders who once felt disconnected—and discover how they became champions of safety and change. Their experiences are filled with lessons, and by learning from them, you can avoid setbacks and step straight into your own success story.

Early mornings at the chemical plant were often chaotic, a fact glaringly evident at every shift change. Enter Laura, the operations manager—technically proficient yet emotionally distant, an expert in spreadsheets but a ghost on the production floor. Her reluctance to engage with the shop floor stemmed not from neglect but from a belief that safety was solely the responsibility of the safety department, not hers to lead. Some operators referred to her as "Invisible."

However, everything changed when a minor yet pivotal incident disrupted the plant's daily routine. A newly installed piece of equipment exploded, causing a scare that could have escalated into a catastrophic event had people been nearby. Laura, standing nervously at the fringe of the crowd during the post-incident meeting, listened as stories emerged of near misses and miscommunications leading up to the event. The air was thick with tension and a pressing need for a shift in approach. Laura wasn't aware of the prior challenges because they weren't documented in spreadsheets or the production schedule.

Initially feeling detached, Laura decided to step out from behind her desk, discovering areas of the operation she had never seen before—equipment overdue for replacement and team members she had never met. This eye-opening experience revealed a gap in her understanding of the work environment. Laura came to realize that safety was not a hindrance to productivity but her ally. The safety team, once viewed as obstacles, became crucial partners. Recognizing this misunderstanding was pivotal; from it, she began fostering genuine collaboration and engagement with her team, redefining her approach to leadership.

With this new perspective, Laura initiated regular walkarounds, transforming them into opportunities for meaningful engagement rather than lonely inspections. She actively listened to her team's concerns and ideas, cultivating a culture where safety was a shared responsibility. Her involvement led to a remarkable shift in morale and safety practices, as team members felt empowered to voice concerns and contribute solutions.

Laura's story illustrates that safety is not solely about regulatory compliance; it thrives where every individual feels accountable. Her leadership inspired change, encouraging corporate visitors to engage more genuinely. Instead of flying in for quick, surface-level visits, she urged them to slow down, connect with frontline work, and engage in meaningful safety conversations with her team. Her approach saved lives and fundamentally redefined leadership on her terms.

Laura wasn't the only one. Another leader I know from a different location experienced a similar transformation—a change that not only altered how they viewed safety but also how they led their entire team. Not too long ago—well, maybe a decade ago—Troy was known in the maintenance crew as the quintessential 'keep your head down' type of manager. He navigated daily tasks with efficiency but rarely considered the broader impacts of safety on his team. His operational success hinged on machine uptime and the speed with which issues were resolved, inadvertently leaving a gap in safety engagement.

One frigid winter morning in the heart of the USA, that changed. A routine check-up revealed a critical safety lapse—a malfunctioning protective interlock on one of the high-speed mixers. Despite years of experience, it was a sobering moment for Troy, realizing that while his team kept production running, they were inadvertently gambling with each other's safety. One day, a courageous employee, clearly overwhelmed, rushed up to Troy and blurted out, "You have to get more involved! This is going to kill someone! Why can't you fix this?" The fear and desperation in his voice were impossible to ignore.

Troy's transformation was profound. Shaken, he finally listened—truly listened—to his team for the first time in years. Through candid conversations, he heard their fears and innovative ideas. He realized that leadership wasn't about having all the answers; it was about creating space for the right voices. This realization marked a turning point where the value of listening became his most powerful leadership tool.

Prompted by this revelation, Troy began seeking advice from his team members. Initially skeptical, his crew was surprised by the sudden shift in his demeanor. He asked questions about their routines, potential hazards they noticed, and suggestions for improvements. His genuine curiosity sparked candid conversations. In that moment, Troy realized, *Wow, I haven't really taken the time to listen to these folks in decades.* He understood that the people closest to the work had real concerns—and even better, real ideas about how to make things safer and stronger. It hit him hard:

leadership isn't about having all the answers; it's about creating the space for the right voices to be heard.

Beyond adjusting operational protocols, Troy led a safety-first task force, aiming to root out complacency and embed safety into every maintenance routine. He introduced collaborative risk assessments and peer-review checklists, ensuring team members cross-examined each other's safety measures—a small step that significantly improved accountability and vigilance.

Within months, the maintenance team evolved into a collaborative environment where proactively addressing potential hazards became the norm. Word spread quickly across departments, as other team leaders marveled at the maintenance crew's newfound attention to safety and mutual support.

Troy's journey from a detached manager to a proactive safety champion underscores a crucial lesson: when leaders prioritize safety and engage their teams, they cultivate an environment where every member feels responsible for not only their own safety but also for each other's. In Troy's case, an unheralded transformation translated into resiliency built on mutual trust and continuous improvement.

This brings us to one of the core traits all effective safety leaders share: trust. Trust is fundamental in fostering an effective and resilient culture within organizations, serving as the very bedrock upon which successful leadership is constructed. Let's explore why trust is indispensable and how leaders can actively cultivate it.

Engaged leadership is not just pivotal; it is the driving force behind a successful organization. Leaders who actively participate in safety initiatives foster an environment where safety becomes a shared value, deeply embedded in the organizational fabric. By embracing their role and demonstrating genuine commitment, leaders inspire others to prioritize safety, transforming it from a checklist item to a core aspect of everyday operations.

Having explored transformative stories of leaders like Laura and Troy, what lessons can we extract about the characteristics of engaged safety leaders? These leaders make a noticeable impact by embodying key traits that encourage safety excellence as natural as breathing. Let's dive into these characteristics:

Engaged leaders ensure clarity in conversations. They facilitate two-way dialogues that align vision, energize action, and eliminate ambiguity. By clearly painting the picture and being open to feedback, they unify everyone on the path forward.

Effective leaders understand that forming a well-rounded perspective relies on seeking diverse viewpoints. By actively encouraging varied opinions, they avoid being swayed by a single narrative. This approach involves engaging with individuals across different roles and experiences, listening to diverse insights before arriving at a conclusion. Such practice enriches their understanding and fosters an inclusive environment where every voice feels valued and heard.

In any thriving business, leaders recognize that leveraging diverse perspectives is integral across all areas, not just in safety. By embracing this philosophy throughout their operations, they ensure the business functions as a 'well-oiled machine.' Seeking varied opinions allows for a more comprehensive understanding of challenges and opportunities, fostering innovation and adaptability. This mindset transforms leadership from decision-making based on solitary views to strategies built on collective wisdom, ensuring robust, resilient, and responsive business practices.

They often set aside hierarchical barriers and engage in discussions that energize and empower employees. Great leaders don't just share ideas—they invite others into their vision. They know that people can't read minds, so they avoid vague terms and do not leave things open to interpretation. Instead, engaged leaders paint the full picture. They ask thoughtful questions, listen deeply, and take the time to explain their own thinking clearly. Every conversation feels like a two-way street rather than a monologue. And the best part? Everyone walks away knowing exactly what to do next—energized, aligned, and ready to move forward.

Empathy is another defining trait. Effective safety leaders empathize with their team, understanding the pressures and challenges they face on the ground. They recognize that safety isn't just about compliance with rules but also about concern for their colleagues' well-being. When workers see leadership that values their safety as a personal commitment rather than an operational necessity, a profound shift in culture occurs.

In Bob Edwards' "Bob's Guide to Operational Learning," the concept of industrial empathy emerges as a pivotal theme. This concept is defined as the ability of leaders and management within industrial settings to understand and empathize with the frontline workers' experiences, challenges, and perspectives. Industrial empathy goes beyond compliance with safety regulations; it requires a cultural shift towards genuine understanding and trust-building between management and employees.

A compelling literary example that encapsulates these principles can be found in Harper Lee's "To Kill a Mockingbird." In this classic novel, Atticus Finch, a lawyer and father, embodies empathy and understanding, transcending societal norms for the greater good. His approach parallels industrial empathy in essence, offering a powerful illustration of how empathy can drive transformative outcomes.

Atticus Finch exemplifies the key elements of safety leadership and empathy through his integrity, moral courage, and attentive listening. In defending Tom Robinson, Finch prioritizes understanding and justice over societal pressures, mirroring leaders who truly listen and act with moral resolve, inspiring trust and commitment across their teams and transforming traditional compliance into a belief of shared safety and accountability.

Moreover, Finch's integrity and courage underscore the importance of ethical leadership. Leaders in industries are encouraged to act not just within regulatory constraints but to be guided by a moral compass that values each worker's life and dignity. This approach aligns perfectly with the concept of moving from compliance to trust, advocating for a culture rooted in empathy and genuine concern for worker well-being.

Through Bob Edwards' framework in "Bob's Guide to Operational Learning," the integration of industrial empathy reshapes organizational culture. Leaders are called to actively listen to their workers, understand the conditions they face, and engage them in creating safer workplaces. This change in dynamics not only improves safety outcomes but also enhances job satisfaction and reduces turnover, driving transformative results across the organization.

Atticus Finch's narrative offers a literary parallel that emphasizes empathy as a catalyst for change. Just as Finch's unwavering belief in equality and justice creates ripples in his community, industrial empathy leads to profound and positive changes in workplace safety. The story inspires leaders to adopt a holistic approach that values human connection and understanding as core components of effective safety leadership.

Engaged safety leaders are visible. Visibility in leadership, especially within culture, goes beyond physical presence—it's about being an accessible, consistent, and integral part of the daily work environment. Leaders who practice visibility actively engage with their teams, ensuring that safety remains a prominent and non-negotiable priority.

A leader's visibility is amplified by their consistent presence. Being present on the floor and engaging with team members regularly enhances accessibility and demonstrates a tangible commitment to safety. Leaders who are frequently seen and approachable create an environment where employees feel comfortable communicating safety concerns, thereby reducing barriers to open dialogue and trust.

Visible leaders serve as role models. When leaders visibly adhere to safety protocols and actively participate in safety discussions and exercises, they set a standard for the team. This modeling provides a practical demonstration of safety priorities, reinforcing the leader's commitment to safety and inspiring the same level of dedication in their team.

Being visible allows leaders to witness operations firsthand and gather real-time feedback. This situational awareness enables quicker responses to safety concerns and facilitates immediate corrective actions, demonstrating the leader's proactive stance on safety. By observing their team in action, leaders can also identify potential safety improvements and show their commitment to fostering a safer workplace.

The ongoing presence of a leader helps build strong, trust-based relationships. When leaders genuinely engage with their teams, understanding personal and professional challenges, they earn respect and loyalty. This relational strength encourages a culturally ingrained safety mindset, where team members feel valued and responsible for both their own and their colleagues' safety.

Through visibility, leaders send a powerful message: safety is important enough to demand their personal involvement. This influential visibility shapes how safety is perceived and prioritized within an organization, illustrating that leadership is about leading the charge on the front lines of safety, not operating from behind a desk.

Such leaders consistently hold themselves accountable for safety outcomes, taking personal responsibility rather than shifting blame. They set clear expectations and model the behavior they wish to see. By doing so, they establish a culture where accountability isn't feared but embraced as a mutual commitment to safety excellence. To truly influence and foster safety excellence, effective leaders begin by holding themselves accountable, embodying the principle of looking in the mirror before assessing others. This reflective approach is not an exercise in humility but a strategic practice that shapes leadership effectiveness and integrity.

The practice of self-reflection underscores the importance of introspection in leadership. Leaders who pause to evaluate their own contributions to workplace culture set a precedent for personal responsibility. This involves critically examining their actions and decisions to understand how they may influence team dynamics and safety outcomes.

For instance, a leader reflecting on a recent safety lapse might ask, "What could I have done differently to prevent this situation?" By starting with such introspection, leaders demonstrate humility and a genuine commitment to self-improvement, which resonates powerfully with their teams.

By prioritizing accountability, leaders set a powerful example for the entire organization. Employees notice that their leaders are willing to take responsibility for mistakes, encouraging them to adopt similar standards. Leaders who admit their errors and learn from them demonstrate resilience and growth, reinforcing a culture of continuous improvement.

This self-accountability fosters a culture of transparency. When leaders openly practice self-reflection, they create a communicative environment where employees feel empowered to voice concerns and share feedback without fear of negative repercussions. Transparency at the leadership level establishes a tone of sincerity and trust throughout the organization.

Self-accountable leaders transform safety into an organizational value rather than a hierarchical mandate. By introspectively assessing their contributions to both successes and failures, they promote a framework where safety is viewed as a shared responsibility, encouraging team members to actively participate in maintaining and enhancing safety standards.

In essence, when leaders take time to 'look in the mirror,' they model the humility and accountability they hope to see in their teams—transforming safety from a set of rules into a shared commitment.

Trust is the foundation of psychological safety. When leaders act with transparency and consistency, they create an environment where employees can express concerns, collaborate freely, and innovate— enhancing both safety and creativity. In trust-rich environments, teams feel empowered and engaged, driving a culture that supports open communication and mutual respect.

Assurance enhances communication across all organizational levels. In a high-trust environment, leaders and employees engage in meaningful, candid exchanges. These dialogues empower workers to share insights and suggestions confidently, contributing to a vibrant safety conversation where information flows freely. Clear communication supports the prompt identification and resolution of safety concerns, ultimately leading to a safer work environment.

When confidence is established, it fosters a collective commitment to shared safety goals. Leaders who trust their teams and are trusted in return galvanize a unified effort toward maintaining a safe workspace. Collaborative initiatives become easier to introduce and sustain as employees take ownership of safety practices, recognizing their role in the collective mission.

During times of organizational change or following safety incidents, trust serves as a stabilizing force. Trusted leaders can guide their teams smoothly through transitions, as their intentions and directives are seen as credible and in the best interest of everyone involved. Trust not only facilitates the implementation of new safety protocols but also helps maintain morale and cooperation during potentially turbulent periods.

Trust, therefore, is not a supplementary trait for leaders; it is essential for cultivating a thriving culture. When leaders prioritize building and maintaining trust, they empower their organizations to flourish, continuously improve, and safeguard the well-being of every member.

These key traits of engaged safety leaders facilitate a thriving culture and underscore an important truth: effective leadership transforms safety from a compliance-focused activity into a core organizational value, seamlessly integrated into everyday workflow. Engaged leaders lead by example, igniting a shared commitment to safety that becomes intrinsic to the organization.

Now, as we transition, consider how these characteristics shape systemic changes within organizations. How can we encourage more leaders to embrace these crucial elements and catalyze a culture of safety beyond compliance?

You've already met Laura and Troy—two leaders who discovered the power of true engagement and meaningful conversations with their teams.

Now, take a moment to reflect: what kind of conversations are you having with those doing the real work? Grab a pen and jot down the steps you're taking today. Think of the moment when Laura walked the floor and Troy listened deeply—what similar opportunity is in front of you? As we progress, we'll explore how asking the right curious questions can open doors to changes you never imagined. Let's continue on this journey!

CHAPTER 9:
MASTERING SAFETY CONVERSATIONS

"The only true wisdom is in knowing you know nothing."
– Socrates

Have you ever noticed what happens when a leader addresses an employee about safety? Too often, it becomes a one-sided interaction—a brief nod or silent adjustment, like pushing down a face shield without a word exchanged. I've seen leaders approach workers, make quick corrections, and walk away, believing they've done something beneficial. Yet, employees' expressions often reveal frustration or embarrassment—not because safety doesn't matter to them, but because they weren't engaged in dialogue.

This silent correction routine highlights a larger issue: it undermines trust. When actions replace conversation, it diminishes opportunities for learning and improvement, turning what should be a collaborative effort into a missed chance for connection and understanding. Instead of fostering a culture of shared safety, this approach erodes the very trust needed to sustain it.

Consider one powerful image: pointing to your eyes to signal missing safety glasses without saying anything. While well-intentioned, this nonverbal correction lacks context and engagement, failing to build a collaborative environment where safety is everyone's responsibility. I have even heard seasoned consultants explain that this kind of quick, nonverbal correction is the key to building an ownership culture. While I understand the intent, I believe we need to look deeper.

Real ownership doesn't stem from silent signals alone. It flourishes through genuine, intentional conversations—the kind that require time, trust, and care.

If you want a culture where people genuinely look out for each other—not just because they have to, but because they want to—you *can't shortcut the process*. You have to earn it.

You must create an atmosphere where feedback feels like support, not criticism. Where reminders are received with gratitude, not resentment. Once you've built that foundation of trust, a simple point and a smile can convey everything needed.

But without trust? It risks becoming just another gesture that goes unnoticed—or worse, breeds frustration.

So, I ask you—and I ask myself—what is the goal? Are we teaching leaders how to correct behavior? Or are we teaching them how to build culture? The difference matters.

The culture we create will reflect the approach we choose today.

Here's the truth: Safety isn't just about compliance. It's about connection. Safety isn't something we do to people; it's something we build with them. A real conversation—a moment of respect, a moment of caring, a moment of trust, a moment of empathy—can make all the difference.

It's not about swooping in to fix someone; it's about standing beside them, asking curious questions, listening, and collaborating toward something greater.

Imagine if, instead of a silent adjustment or a quick lecture, we approached with genuine curiosity: "Hey, how's the work going today? Is there anything making it tough to stay safe?" or "I noticed your face shield—can we chat about it for a second?"

In that moment, you're not just reminding them to be safe; you're showing them they matter. You're building trust. You're reinforcing a culture where safety is everyone's priority because everyone feels ownership in it. Small conversations build great cultures—one respectful moment at a time.

Every interaction is a choice:

Will we lecture?

Or will we lead?

The culture we build for tomorrow starts with the conversations we're having today. **It's that simple—and that powerful.**

So, what makes a conversation truly meaningful? How do we move beyond quick reminders and into real connections that inspire ownership—where everyone feels responsible for safety and proud of the role they play?

To cultivate a proactive safety mindset, leaders must initiate trust-rich dialogues that go beyond enforcing rules, empowering every team member to own their safety responsibilities. Let's explore this together, for when we understand the dynamics of a great conversation, we unlock the door to a stronger, safer workplace—one where every voice matters.

But here's the deeper truth: trust isn't something that happens overnight. It's nurtured and carefully crafted through every word we speak and every interaction we have. If we're genuinely committed to moving beyond the surface level of safety compliance, we need to change how we approach our conversations with our teams.

Reflect for a moment: *how often do we truly take the time to listen and invite others into the dialogue?* The conversations we have can either build a strong foundation of trust or leave it fragile and unsteady. So how do we initiate conversations that not only inform but actually **inspire ownership, spark accountability, and strengthen trust**?

To transform these initial insights into meaningful actions, a structured roadmap is essential. Let's explore six foundational steps to cultivate a culture rooted in trust and collective responsibility. By following this practical guide, we can move beyond theory to create a dynamic workplace where every voice counts.

Step 1: Building Rapport and Establishing Trust: The Cornerstones of Safety Conversations

Creating an atmosphere of trust begins with simple, open-ended questions that demonstrate genuine interest in team members. Asking, "How are you doing?" or "What do you enjoy most about your work here?" bridges the gap between leaders and employees, inviting dialogue beyond immediate work concerns. This approach values individuals beyond their roles, fostering an environment where every voice feels heard and respected. As rapport strengthens, conversations naturally evolve into meaningful exchanges that empower team members to actively participate in safety dialogues and collective problem-solving.

Adapting your approach to building rapport is crucial for effective communication and leadership. Different situations call for varying styles of engagement, depending on your familiarity with the employee. For new team members, establishing an open and welcoming introduction is vital, while with longstanding colleagues, the focus might shift to deepening trust and understanding their evolving perspectives.

Combining work-related questions with personal interests can create a deeper connection and foster trust between leaders and employees. Here's how to blend these topics into natural, engaging conversations for both new and longtime employees:

For New Employees: Imagine meeting a new hire eager to feel part of the team. You approach them during a break and say:

"It's great to have you on board. How has your first week been? Is there anything you need to feel more settled?"

[Pause to listen, then segue into a personal interest] "By the way, do you play any sports or have hobbies you're passionate about? It's nice to find common ground outside of work."

This approach shows professional support and personal interest, helping to build rapport and ease their integration into the team.

For Longtime Employees: Consider connecting with a colleague you've known for years to deepen your relationship:

"Hey, we've been working together for quite some time. I'd love to know what recent changes you've found most impactful and if there's anything new you'd like to tackle."

"And how's your family doing? I remember you mentioning your daughter was starting school—how's that going?"

This method strengthens trust by recognizing contributions and showing genuine interest in personal lives, enhancing their sense of belonging and satisfaction in the workplace.

By starting every conversation with a focus on rapport and trust, you set the stage for meaningful safety dialogues. When team members feel heard, they're more likely to speak up—laying the groundwork for deeper exploration in the next step.

Step 2: Understanding Challenges: Uncovering Safety Insights Through Open Dialogue

Every organization is a dynamic ecosystem where the daily rhythms of employees significantly shape its atmosphere. Central to a thriving culture is the leader's willingness to dive deeply into these everyday experiences, embracing both successes and challenges. Encouraging team members to share their day-to-day narratives is not just a form of active listening; it is a strategic approach to uncovering critical insights that might otherwise remain hidden in the noise of routine operations.

When leaders ask questions like, "What's the best part of your job?" or "What are the toughest challenges you face?" they aren't just engaging in small talk. Instead, these queries elicit comprehensive, insightful responses that paint a vivid picture of an employee's work environment. Such questions invite workers to reflect on their roles, revealing operational hurdles that could influence task efficiency and safety protocols. More importantly, these conversations provide employees with a platform to voice their opinions, fostering respect and community.

These discussions go beyond rules, and regulatory obligations; they reveal blind spots in safety practices that routine reports often miss. By truly understanding what challenges your team faces, you uncover risks and initiate practical improvements. This approach transforms regular dialogue into strategic alliances that enhance safety.

Furthermore, understanding these challenges allows for a dynamic feedback loop where safety measures can be continuously refined and adapted. It repositions leaders from enforcers of safety protocols to co-collaborators in creating robust, worker-informed safety procedures. This realignment not only boosts morale but also fosters shared responsibility for safety, where each team member feels invested in and accountable for the well-being of the collective.

In essence, unpacking the stories behind daily challenges enriches the organization's understanding of its operational environment, illuminating paths to a safer and more cohesive workplace. This holistic approach bridges the gap between leadership intentions and the lived experiences of those on the ground, underscoring the essential role of conversation in driving continuous safety improvements.

Step 3: Exploring Safety with Intent: Unveiling Hazards through Inquiry

Transitioning into discussions centered around safety while maintaining intentionality is crucial in crafting an environment attentive to potential hazards and necessary preventative measures. This approach involves moving beyond surface-level interactions to engage in a dialogue that truly scrutinizes the safety landscape within the workplace.

Questions like, "What should someone know to safely perform your job?" or "How might someone get injured in this role?" serve as catalysts for deep reflection. They guide team members to introspectively consider their daily routines, revealing subtle patterns that might contribute to safety risks. Engaging employees this way brings their expertise to the forefront, tapping into their firsthand experiences and insights.

Picture a leader on the manufacturing floor, genuinely curious about the workers' experience. By asking, "How might someone get injured in this role?" they invite insights that traditional safety audits might miss. For instance, a manager's question like this uncovered a longstanding issue with a slippery floor area. Workers had known about the hazard but hadn't reported it, assuming it was a low priority. Encouraged by the direct question, they voiced their concerns, leading to immediate improvements and illustrating the power of conversational inquiries to surface unseen risks and foster a shared safety responsibility.

The effectiveness of this discussion relies on illustrating risks from the perspective of those most familiar with the tasks at hand. Such perspectives are invaluable because they often capture nuances that broad safety policies might overlook. The depth of understanding gained through these conversations allows leaders to tailor safety protocols to the organization's real-world challenges, enhancing the overall safety net.

Moreover, engaging employees with thoughtful inquiries makes them feel valued contributors rather than a cog in the wheel. Encouraging them to share what they observe daily turns safety into a shared endeavor rather than an imposed task. When workers are involved in discussions about hazards, their ownership of safety strengthens, fostering a collaborative environment where vigilance becomes everyone's responsibility.

In essence, exploring safety with intent transforms routine safety checks into thoughtful, ongoing dialogues that surface critical insights. This ongoing engagement is pivotal not only in preventing incidents but also in cultivating a workplace where safety becomes an intrinsic part of the company's ideology. The dialogue must continuously evolve, incorporating new information and adapting to changing work conditions to maintain its relevance and effectiveness.

Step 4: Evaluating Risks and Controls: The Heartbeat of Safety Conversations

Imagine standing on the factory floor, the buzz of machinery a constant hum in the background. In this environment, it's easy to view safety protocols as just another task on a long list of "to-dos." Yet, when you pause to step into a conversation about risks and controls, you're not just ticking boxes on a safety checklist—you're engaging in a vital dialogue that could make the difference between safety and catastrophe.

Each discussion on risk evaluation and control measures can transform abstract concepts into actionable insights. When you initiate discussions about potential injuries and existing controls, you're doing more than following protocol; you're engaging your team in a critical thinking exercise with real-world implications. Asking questions like, "How can someone get injured in this role?" focuses attention on potential hazards, paving the way for innovation in safety practices.

Picture a conversation where the team closely examines real risks and the controls designed to prevent them. This is where the real work of safety occurs—not in manuals, but in meaningful dialogue. Here, leaders and team members must create a vivid picture of the current safety landscape. Reflect on this pivotal question: "How bad might the injury be?" This question serves a dual purpose—it prompts a candid assessment of potential hazards and encourages team members to visualize the gravity of the associated risks. Allowing these risks to be verbalized often results in profound 'light bulb' moments that deepen understanding and trigger proactive improvements.

Team members' grasp of engineering controls, administrative measures, and preventive strategies come alive in these dialogues. Such conversations expose both the strengths and gaps in current safety practices, inviting team members to share their insights and, importantly, their concerns. This engagement is essential—who better to understand the potential pitfalls than those who navigate them daily?

For leaders, this dialogue presents an opportunity to verify and refine safety controls, ensuring they serve as effective tools in preserving health and safety rather than remaining theoretical constructs. It empowers leaders to make informed decisions about adjustments and enhancements. It also reveals whether training is effective—can the team comprehend all controls beyond the PPE typically highlighted by leaders?

Ultimately, these conversations illustrate a profound truth: effective safety measures are not dictated by top-down mandates but are crafted through active collaboration and continuous feedback. By embedding this practice into the fabric of your organization, you foster an environment where safety becomes everyone's responsibility, not just a managerial directive. Each conversation is a heartbeat, reaffirming your collective commitment to a safer workplace. Through these engaged interactions, you cultivate a culture that not only values safety but lives and breathes it every single day.

In these dialogues, as team members articulate possible injuries and recognize current safety protocols, they begin to appreciate the complex tapestry of safety controls, from administrative measures to preventive strategies. Understanding who might endure what kind of harm and how adds layers to the conversation that documentation alone cannot achieve. This not only heightens awareness but also empowers employees, giving them a voice in shaping safer pathways.

By employing questions and reflective thinking similar to the Socratic method, leaders can elevate these discussions from routine safety checks to profound learning experiences. This ancient dialectical method involves posing insightful questions that lead participants to discover answers themselves, rather than simply being told what to do. In a safety context, it's about guiding employees to uncover deeper truths about their roles and responsibilities. By asking, "What do these potential risks tell us about our safety practices?" or "How can we further mitigate these dangers?" the conversation progresses beyond compliance and towards enlightenment.

Envision a bustling factory setting where safety protocols often merge into the everyday hum. A leader pauses amidst this activity to ask, "How bad might the injury be if something goes wrong here?" This question doesn't just follow procedure—it opens a dialogue that transforms understanding. When a supervisor posed this question during a safety briefing, it sparked a discussion about emergency shut-off access, prompting a redesign to prevent simple mishaps from escalating. These conversations, grounded in real scenarios, ensure that safety controls are not solely theoretical but actively refined tools for maintaining workplace safety. Through such dialogue, safety becomes not just a task but a shared commitment, strengthening the organization's core.

Such inquiry cultivates critical thinking and inspires deeper engagement with safety principles. As team members participate in these structured discussions, they become co-creators of a culture that is reflexive and responsive. The process transforms individuals from passive participants into active contributors in crafting an environment where safety isn't just an obligation but a collective commitment.

In summary, evaluating risks and controls through open dialogue, guided by Socratic questioning, is not only about mitigating immediate dangers. It is about building a coherent safety ecosystem where each voice contributes to a tapestry of proactive vigilance and continuous improvement. This approach enriches the safety landscape, fostering an atmosphere where enlightenment leads to safer, more aware workplaces.

Step 5: Encourage Collaborative Solutions: Empowering Team Engagement

Imagine a workplace where every team member's voice is not only heard but celebrated—a place where everyone feels integral to the safety solution. Involving those doing the work may hold the key to maximizing safety effectiveness; it's in these collaborative spaces that true innovation occurs.

When potential risks or hazards arise, the typical response might be to solve them through a top-down directive. But what if we flipped the script? Instead of assuming solutions, why not ask your team: "If resources were available, how would you address this issue?" This simple, empowering question transforms the dynamic, inviting team members into the decision-making process. It's a subtle shift that communicates, "We value your expertise and insights."

During these moments of genuine inquiry, solutions emerge that are practical and field-tested, while team members begin to feel a sense of ownership over the outcomes. This sense of responsibility fosters a commitment that transcends departmental boundaries and titles, uniting everyone under shared safety goals.

As discussed, using Socratic questioning encourages ownership. At this stage, it helps the team dig deeper into potential solutions rather than settling for surface fixes.

These dialogues are not just about finding solutions to immediate problems; they're about elevating the entire team's capacity to think critically, draw upon collective wisdom, and innovate continuously. Each conversation becomes a canvas where ideas are painted, tested, and refined collectively. Through collaborative problem-solving, teams don't solely comply with safety protocols—they embody them, living and breathing a dynamic and resilient safety culture.

The call to action is clear: engage, empower, and evolve. By inviting your team into the dialogue and leveraging the power of collaboration, you not only address today's challenges but also lay the groundwork for a safer, more united future. Let's turn collaborative conversations into a cornerstone of safety culture, one open-ended question at a time, fueling a workplace where everyone feels empowered to contribute to a safer environment.

Step 6: Commitment and Follow-Up: Solidifying the Bonds of Culture through Trust

Meet Joe, a dedicated manager who believed he had a firm grasp on his team's operations. It wasn't until he witnessed a casual conversation between the Director of Safety and his crew that he realized the hidden risks lurking in their daily routines. The Director asked, "What challenges do you face that I might not see?" The insights uncovered were profound, prompting a deeper understanding of the hurdles his team encountered. This dialogue marked the beginning of a transformative journey, emphasizing the power of open communication in fostering a culture of safety where everyone feels accountable.

The next day, several employees eagerly approached the Director during his walkthrough with Joe. They shared more insights about the challenges they faced, and some even proposed straightforward solutions that required only a few minutes of constructive conversation to plan or implement.

With Joe's experience as a backdrop, let's explore how leaders can cultivate a culture where proactive safety becomes a cornerstone of team dynamics through visible commitment and engagement.

Imagine leaving a conversation with the feeling that you've started something significant—little ripples in a pond that could lead to substantial waves of change. That's the power of concluding your safety dialogues with commitment and follow-up. These final steps are not just a closing act; they are the cement that binds a cohesive ownership culture securely in place.

As these impactful conversations draw to a close, encourage a mutual commitment to action and improvement. It's an invitation for each participant to uphold their part in the safety net that binds your team together. "Could you share these new insights with your colleagues?" Such a prompt encourages knowledge sharing and plants the seeds of advocacy, turning insights into a rallying cry for broader safety awareness across the organization.

Remember, commitment without follow-up is simply an empty promise. By revisiting unresolved issues or checking the progress on discussed initiatives, leaders underscore their dedication to genuine safety improvements. Imagine how it feels for a team member when a leader circles back to a previously mentioned concern—it reinforces a promise; it's saying, "**What you shared matters.**"

When leaders circle back, they demonstrate they're truly listening. Follow-up turns promises into progress—and that's how trust takes root.

Transformation in safety begins with leadership that embraces action through conversation and collaboration. By engaging the team with clear, consistent communication and regular follow-ups, leaders reinforce the idea that safety is a collective commitment. It's about building trust and fostering a workplace where safety is everyone's passion.

As a leader, your task is to integrate these actions into all safety discussions and commitment exercises. The journey is ongoing, elevating safety conversations into continuous learning and improvement opportunities.

Engage, listen, and inspire your team, championing a culture where every voice matters and safety is genuinely a shared responsibility.

Consider how these conversational techniques can extend beyond safety—enhancing your approach to audits, inspections, and team communications. Explore how these practices can transform the way your entire business operates, shifting the focus from blindly following rules to steering your company with purpose and care. Ready to embark on this transformative journey? Let's dig deeper into team dynamics and operational improvement in the next chapter!

CHAPTER 10:
GAME CHANGING AUDITS

"Tell me and I forget. Teach me and I may remember. Involve me and I learn."
-Benjamin Franklin

Have you ever considered how you feel when you hear the word "audit"? Is it an opportunity to gather insights or just another checklist to complete? Traditional audits often overlook the voices that truly matter—the frontline employees who experience daily operations firsthand. They understand where the real gaps lie, beyond what's simply documented.

In a conventional audit, the process typically focuses on compliance checks and paperwork. Imagine an audit at a manufacturing plant where the auditor spends most of their time in the office, reviewing safety manuals, ticking boxes on safety protocol sheets, and conducting brief interviews with the safety manager. Frontline workers rarely have a chance to share their everyday experiences. Consequently, the audit may confirm compliance with established safety procedures but might miss nuanced operational challenges and potential hazards that workers encounter daily.

Now, contrast this with a more interactive audit approach. At a similar manufacturing plant, the auditor starts their day on the factory floor, engaging directly with employees. They initiate open conversations with machine operators and line workers, asking questions like, "What safety challenges do you face here?" and "Have you encountered any close calls recently?" During these discussions, a worker reveals that a specific piece of equipment often jams, creating a potential safety risk. This insight, which traditional audits might overlook, prompts immediate action to address the hazard. The audit evolves into a dialogue that not only evaluates compliance but also enhances culture by valuing and acting upon employee feedback.

Let's explore how curiosity-driven conversations, rather than checklists and policies, can transform audits into powerful tools for improvement. Engaging diverse voices and understanding the lived experiences on the ground can unlock insights crucial for enhancing workplace safety. When audits prioritize dialogue with those in the trenches, they shift from routine procedures to catalysts for positive change and resilience. By embracing this approach, we can view audits as pathways to a safer, more cohesive workplace.

I'm talking about real, genuine human conversations — with the people turning wrenches, operating cranes, climbing ladders, and supervising teams. The magic of learning doesn't happen on paper; it occurs in the field, with people. Let's explore why and how engaging conversations can supercharge your audits and mindset:

Step 1: Start with genuine curiosity, not an agenda. Before stepping onto the floor or into a maintenance bay, leave the clipboard mentality behind. Instead, bring one simple thing: curiosity. Ask yourself:

"What can I learn today?"

"What would it be like to do their job for a day?"

"What pressures or barriers might they be facing?"

This shift in mindset transforms you from an "auditor" or "finder of mistakes" into a partner in safety through collaboration with the facility.

People open up to those who are curious—not to someone solely looking for mistakes or gaps!

Step 2: Talk with people, not at them. When you meet a technician, line operator, or supervisor, don't start with "Where's your permit?" Instead, say:

"Can you walk me through how you approach [this task] safely?"

"What's the trickiest part about keeping this job safe?"

"What do you wish leadership understood about this process?"

You'll hear stories, not just answers—stories about real risks, smart adaptations, and insights a document can't provide. That's where the richest learning exists in every facility.

Step 3: When someone shares a solution they've developed—a safer method, a smart tweak to a system, or an effective workaround—respond with genuine recognition and enthusiasm. By highlighting these innovations, you build trust and pave the way for further improvements. Embracing what's working well is just as vital as preventing harm, nurturing an atmosphere where positive practices are celebrated and shared.

Step 4: Listen between the lines. Sometimes what people don't say is just as powerful. You might sense hesitations, notice a glance at a broken tool that hasn't been replaced, or hear a technician shrug off a shortcut as "just the way it is."

Curiosity means being attuned to the unsaid. You're not just listening for compliance; you're identifying pressure points, pain points, and passion points.

I've seen it happen countless times — auditors running through a checklist, rattling off questions without even looking up at the person across from them. And that's the issue: they're talking at someone, not engaging in a conversation. There's a significant difference!

Active listening allows you to pick up on cues that often go unnoticed in checklist mode—hesitations, gestures, or glances toward a problem. These moments can reveal the real story.

Have you ever witnessed this pattern, or maybe even found yourself in it? It serves as a powerful reminder that true connection, even in an audit, opens the door to understanding far beyond a simple list of yes or no answers.

Step 5: Close conversations with empowerment, not judgment. At the end of your discussion, express your gratitude. Thank them sincerely and let them know their insights are shaping a safer, stronger workplace — not just filling out an audit form.

"You've given me so much to think about. You're helping us build a system that truly works for the people who use it."

People remember how you made them feel. If they sense judgment, they may shut down next time. If they feel heard, they'll engage more deeply — perhaps even share ideas that could transform the entire program.

Step 6: Reflect: Are you auditing the system alone — or the people too? After you leave the floor, ask yourself:

"Did I learn something today that I couldn't have found in a document?" "Did I gain a better understanding of the human reality of the work?" "Did my questions encourage reflection, or did they provoke defensiveness?"

Here's the truth: strong safety systems aren't built by enforcing rules — they're built by empowering people. Empowerment begins with curiosity and leads to ownership and accountability.

Now that we've explored how curiosity and connection can reshape audit conversations, let's examine what this looks like in practice. Here's a side-by-side comparison of a traditional audit versus a curiosity-driven approach.

Before: Traditional Audit Style (Document-heavy, rigid checklist, minimal human engagement)

Audit Item: Machine Guarding Compliance

- Guard installed per specification
- Guard free of defects and secured properly
- Guard does not impede operation
- Lockout procedure posted nearby

Comments: _____

Typical auditor behavior:

- Stands at a distance, clipboard in hand.
- Asks to see the posted lockout procedure.
- Checks the physical condition of the guard.
- Moves to the next item without engaging the operator.

Outcome: Surface-level compliance check with minimal understanding of real-world challenges.

After: Curiosity-Driven, People-First Audit (Conversation-focused, human-centered, discovery-rich)

Focus Area: Machine Guarding and Real-World Use

Opening Conversation Starters:

- "Can you demonstrate how you interact with this machine during your shift?"
- "Has the guard ever hindered your work? How do you handle that?"
- "If something jams or breaks, what's the first step you take before addressing it?"
- "When did you last see someone need to adjust or remove the guard? What occurred?"
- "What would you change about this setup?"

Field Notes (instead of checklist):

- An operator indicated that guard removal is sometimes necessary during maintenance tasks, but the lockout steps aren't practical in urgent situations.
- A supervisor noted an ongoing backlog for guard repairs due to delays in spare parts.
- Observed operators using personal lockout tags in a way that deviates from the posted procedure, reflecting strong personal ownership but low procedural alignment.

Auditor Reflection Prompt:

- "What insights did I gain today that challenge or conflict with the written procedures?"
- "What barriers are individuals facing that the system doesn't address?"
- "How can we design safer systems with their input, rather than just for them?"

Outcome: In-depth understanding of the gaps between "the manual" and "the real world." Enhanced trust. Opportunities for meaningful, frontline-driven improvements.

To illustrate the difference between a traditional document checklist audit and a curiosity-driven, conversation-based approach, I have included a simple comparison.

Traditional Audit	Curiosity-Driven Audit
Focused on checklists and paperwork	Centered on conversations and context
Auditor remains an observer	Auditor acts as a learner and partner
Evaluates compliance	Explores barriers and real-world adaptations
Reviews procedures	Engages with frontline voices
Focuses on faults and gaps	Seeks collaborative solutions
Yields surface-level insights	Uncovers deeper cultural patterns

The most exciting part? You don't have to choose between structured and curiosity-driven audits—combining both delivers the best of both worlds. By integrating traditional methods with open dialogue and employee engagement, you achieve the structure you need and the insights you want. This hybrid approach transforms routine audits into dynamic tools for improvement, fostering a workplace ripe for growth, innovation, and safety.

Regardless of the audit style you choose, it's crucial that the findings are presented in a way that genuinely helps people learn and grow—not just points out problems. The goal is to ensure that the same gaps don't happen again.

Imagine reading an audit report and encountering the finding: "Replace guard on tank TL-110." Now, put yourself in the shoes of the person responsible for taking action. Without specifics, the team may be left guessing—and that's when critical risks can be overlooked.

While inspecting TL-110, the missing guard over the agitator was immediately noted. Initially, it seemed like a maintenance oversight, but further inquiries revealed the real story. The guard had been removed for maintenance, but an urgent call led the technician away, leaving the agitator unprotected. As time passed and shifts changed, the risk went unnoticed.

This isn't just about replacing a guard; it illustrates how easily safety gaps form when urgent issues overshadow critical follow-up. Immediate action involves securing the guard, but the broader lesson is to fortify procedures to ensure that no unfinished task is overlooked amid daily chaos. Strengthening handoff protocols is crucial to prevent such safety risks from recurring.

In environments like ours, "I'll be right back" can easily turn into "I forgot," and that's when accidents happen—accidents we can absolutely prevent with a stronger process and a little more vigilance.

It's also important to remember that the missing guard could have resulted from various circumstances. Whether it was removed for maintenance, damaged and never replaced, or mistakenly deemed unnecessary, the outcome is the same: an unprotected risk that requires deeper understanding.

The missing guard could have been removed for any of the reasons mentioned or others. Whatever the cause, assuming it means missing the opportunity to ask the right questions.

To take this further, in Chapter 7 of *Environmental Health and Safety Audits: A Compendium of Thoughts and Trends*, Lawrence B. Cahill explores a recurring theme: the classic failures auditors often face. His examination highlights the challenges professionals encounter during safety audits, emphasizing the need to shift from a sole focus on compliance to fostering a culture of trust and proactive leadership.

Prior to this transformative shift, audit processes were strictly compliance-driven, relying heavily on checklists and top-down directives, which often overlooked nuanced safety challenges. This oversight is a key point in Cahill's work. He notes that "even well-intentioned audits can fail if they don't focus on people and culture." His observations reveal the necessity for audits to move beyond procedures to genuinely engage with the dynamic realities present on the ground.

Cahill's insights remind us that real breakthroughs occur when audits prioritize the voices of frontline employees, creating an environment where feedback and trust can flourish.

Incorporating these elements leads to more accurate risk identification and transforms safety from a regulatory requirement into a core organizational value. By recognizing this, companies can leverage audits as tools for continuous improvement with everyone sharing responsibility.

Cahill presents a compelling call to action for organizations seeking transformative results in safety leadership. By understanding and addressing classic audit limitations, companies can pave the way toward sustainable safety practices that exceed compliance, fostering a dynamic environment where trust and accountability thrive.

This brings me to my final thought: Documents can outline what's supposed to happen, but true change occurs when we go beyond the written word and engage in meaningful action. People can reveal what's truly happening. Remember, People First – Safety Always!

If you want your audits to drive real improvement — not just check a box — embrace the messy, beautiful, human side of safety. Ask more questions. Listen wholeheartedly. View every conversation as an opportunity to learn, not to judge.

Audits can be more than evaluations—they can be catalysts for change. When you lead with questions, empathy, and curiosity, audits become opportunities to strengthen culture. This chapter illustrates how transitioning from audit-as-inspection to audit-as-conversation enables organizations to uncover hidden insights and foster an environment where safety thrives naturally.

By incorporating frontline voices and focusing on building an environment of trust and engagement, organizations can significantly enhance safety outcomes. In the next chapter, we'll address one of the toughest aspects of cultural change: resistance. We will explore how effective leadership can transform doubt into buy-in, paving the way for genuine, sustainable improvements.

CHAPTER 11:
OVERCOMING RESISTANCE

"The bamboo that bends is stronger than the oak that resists."
— Japanese Proverb

I vividly remember the day we rolled out a new rule requiring reflective vests for all outdoor workers—intended to improve visibility and reduce accidents in high-traffic areas. The reasoning was sound: enhanced visibility to prevent accidents. Yet, the announcement was met with blank stares, folded arms, and murmurs that quickly escalated into loud objections.

"What next? Helmets inside office buildings?" one employee mumbled. Another, a respected veteran among the crew, simply shook his head, muttering about tradition and how the old ways had served well enough. It was clear that this wasn't just a logistical issue; it was a struggle over tradition, identity, and control.

Initially, I felt frustrated by the lack of immediate understanding and acceptance. However, this sentiment quickly shifted to curiosity and respect for what I realized was a deeply rooted workplace culture. I sat down with Bill, our most outspoken foreman, over coffee. Bill was a repository of wisdom about the team's dynamics. His perspective revealed layers of the crew's mindset that a top-down approach could have easily overlooked.

"These vests," Bill explained, "are not just about the fabric or the new rule. It's about feeling sidelined again by another 'higher-up' decision." His words illuminated an important truth: safety measures, however well-intentioned, must be embedded in the culture rather than imposed upon it.

From that point on, my strategy shifted. We organized inclusive meetings where crew members could voice their concerns and suggest compromises. We paired these discussions with safety workshops, showcasing real-life scenarios where increased visibility had prevented accidents. This approach not only acknowledged their expertise but also made them stakeholders in the safety dialogue, transforming passive compliance into active participation.

The turning point came during a site visit when a simple demonstration highlighted the stark visibility difference between the vests against the site's backdrop. The transformation was gradual but consistent. What began as grumbling evolved into grudging acknowledgment and, ultimately, proactive adoption. When I overheard Bill advising a newcomer on the best way to wear his vest for maximum safety, I realized we had achieved not just compliance but a significant cultural shift.

Reflecting on this journey, I understood that overcoming resistance is less about navigating obstacles and more about honoring human concerns. It presents an opportunity to build trust and ensure that safety is not a directive but a shared value.

A powerful real-world example of this shift is the transformation of Alcoa under Paul O'Neill's leadership. His approach demonstrated how a true commitment to trust and safety can reshape an entire organization.

As mentioned previously, when O'Neill became CEO of Alcoa in 1987, he made a bold decision: he would center the company's strategy on worker safety. At first glance, this seemed unusual, even controversial, for a company primarily focused on productivity and profitability. Alcoa was already known for complying with safety regulations, but O'Neill's vision extended beyond compliance—he aimed for zero injuries. Many within the company, as well as investors, were skeptical, questioning whether a focus on safety could tangibly benefit the organization.

O'Neill's strategy for overcoming this resistance involved a complete cultural shift. He began with communication—holding meetings with employees and stakeholders where he passionately articulated his vision and the intrinsic value of world-class safety. He argued that safety was not just a moral imperative but also a pathway to enhance operational excellence, boost morale, and indirectly increase profits.

To embed safety into the organization's DNA, he established systems for real-time data reporting on safety issues. This transparency empowered employees at all levels to take ownership of safety protocols, fostering a bottom-up change initiative rather than a top-down imposition. O'Neill's slogan was simple yet profound: **"If you want to understand how Alcoa is doing, you need to look at our workplace safety figures."**

The resistance began to wane as results became clear. Injury rates plummeted, and the company's financial performance improved significantly. Within a year of O'Neill's emphasis on safety, Alcoa's profits reached record highs. This transformation revealed a direct correlation between a safety-focused culture and organizational performance.

By overcoming initial resistance and fostering trust through safety, O'Neill demonstrated that a commitment to employee well-being can drive both cultural and financial success. This example illustrates how safety can serve as a foundational pillar for innovation and trust within a corporate structure, making safety leadership a catalyst for broader transformative results.

While Alcoa provides a real-world demonstration of effective safety leadership, fiction can also vividly underscore these concepts. The 1993 film Jurassic Park, directed by Steven Spielberg, serves as a cautionary tale about sidelined safety and unchecked ambition. The plot revolves around a groundbreaking theme park featuring cloned dinosaurs, where safety protocols are repeatedly ignored due to excitement, novelty, and ambition.

The central character, John Hammond, the visionary behind Jurassic Park, epitomizes initial resistance to robust safety measures. Driven by the dream of creating a park that pioneers biological wonders, he often overlooks the warning signs presented by his experts. Dr. Ian Malcolm, a mathematician specializing in chaos theory, serves as the narrative's conscience on safety issues. He frequently warns Hammond about the unpredictability of the park's systems and the catastrophic potential of disregarding safety protocols, succinctly capturing this resistance with the line: "Your scientists were so preoccupied with whether they could, they didn't stop to think if they should."

The story contrasts Dr. Malcolm's prescient warnings with Hammond's visionary drive. As the park's systems fail, the ensuing chaos underscores a crucial lesson: safety cannot be sidelined. This collapse profoundly illustrates that safety must evolve beyond compliance, becoming integral to the operation with sustainable innovation.

The film's climax and resolution reinforce the importance of establishing a culture of safety where resistance is actively minimized. As the survivors escape the island, they embody the lessons learned and a newfound commitment to respecting nature's unpredictability. Their transformation reflects the evolution from resistance to embracing comprehensive safety measures that go beyond regulatory compliance.

"Jurassic Park" serves as a compelling example of how overcoming initial resistance is crucial for fostering a resilient culture. The story illustrates the transformation needed to internalize safety as a fundamental aspect of operations rather than an inconvenience, highlighting both the dangers of neglecting safety and the peace of mind that follows its thorough implementation.

Addressing resistance in your workplace, particularly regarding safety, can feel like an uphill battle. You might wonder, "How do I get started with all these naysayers around?" I understand where you're coming from; I've been there too! Let's break it down into actionable steps you can implement today—a blend of short-term wins and a long-term strategy.

Step 1: Understand the Roots

Get Curious, Not Frustrated: When you face pushback, begin by asking questions. What are the underlying concerns or fears? Is it about changes disrupting routines or something deeper, like a loss of control? Understanding these issues is key to fostering empathy and effective planning. Remember, it's not just about vests or helmets; it's about what they symbolize for your team. Here are some actions you can take, along with tips I've learned the hard way.

Action: Spend a few days observing team interactions without making any changes. Take mental notes on discussions, particularly regarding safety protocols or new implementations. Are there any recurring comments or jokes that reveal underlying sentiments?

Tip: Pay close attention to both verbal and non-verbal cues. Body language can convey as much as words.

Action: Schedule one-on-one meetings or small group sessions that encourage open communication. Clearly express your intent to understand their perspectives rather than critique them.

Tip: Reassure them that this isn't about criticism but about gathering insights to make informed decisions. Sometimes, simply knowing their voices are heard can diminish resistance.

Action: During these discussions, ask open-ended questions like "What concerns do you have about the new safety measures?" or "How do you feel these changes might affect your daily work?"

Tip: Avoid defensive responses. Thank them for their input, even if it's critical. This not only builds trust but also encourages more honest feedback.

Action: After your sessions, review your notes to identify common patterns or themes in the feedback. Is it fear of change? Loss of routine? Perceived top-down imposition?

Tip: Use these themes to guide your communication strategy moving forward. Tailoring your approach to specific concerns can effectively counteract resistance.

Action: In your next group meeting, acknowledge their feelings. Communicate what you've heard and clarify these patterns for better understanding.

Tip: This isn't just about being nice—demonstrating that their feedback influences decisions can turn skepticism into support.

Action: Prioritize the issues based on frequency and impact. Which concerns are raised most often? Which ones could derail your initiative if left unaddressed?

Tip: *Address high-priority issues first to show responsiveness and commitment.*

Action: Whether in a presentation, group meeting, or written memo, integrate these insights into your narrative about why changes are necessary and how they will benefit everyone.

Tip: *Use stories or examples from your team to illustrate your points. When people see reflections of their own experiences in your narrative, they are more likely to engage.*

Remember, understanding the roots of resistance isn't about solving every problem immediately; **it's about laying the groundwork for trust and collaboration.** Effective change occurs when people feel included in the process, not sidelined by it.

Step 2: Identify and Mobilize Influencers

Spot the Opinion Leaders: Every group has its natural leaders. They may lack formal titles, but they wield influence.

Action: Observe dynamics in meetings and informal gatherings. Who do people turn to for reassurance or approval before voicing their agreement? These are your key influencers. Approach them personally and discuss the benefits of the new measures in a way that resonates. Consider sharing a story about how similar changes have been successful elsewhere.

Identify Styles and Preferences: Each influencer has a distinct style. Some are data-driven, while others prioritize relationships. Recognize these patterns.

Action: Engage in one-on-one conversations. Start with casual check-ins to gauge their thoughts on ongoing operations and changes. What concerns them, and what excites them?

Turn Resistance into Alliance:

For instance, Bill—the respected foreman—holds sway over the team. Involve him as an advisory voice on your safety committee. His support can influence the team more effectively than any email or memo.

Delegate Leadership:

Once trust is established, empower these influencers to lead peer discussions. Their endorsement will create a ripple effect.

Action: Involve them in pilot programs or feedback sessions, allowing them to speak first in group meetings to guide the narrative and dynamics from within.

Valuing their Input:

Appreciate their perspectives and leverage their feedback. This not only influences them but also affects everyone they impact.

Action: Develop initiatives based on their suggestions, and publicly acknowledge their contributions and the positive changes they inspire.

Creating a Shared Vision:

Align your change goals with their personal or team objectives.

Action: Create a shared roadmap that clarifies their roles and how these connect to the larger picture. Use visuals or flowcharts to demonstrate how their involvement leads to broader operational successes.

I understand the skepticism—because I once felt it too. Before entering the world of safety leadership, I didn't always grasp the bigger picture. That experience allows me to relate to today's influencers and guide them with empathy, not ego.

Step 3: Communicate the "Why"

Effectively communicating the "why" behind culture improvements is essential for shifting mindsets and gaining buy-in from your team. Let's explore how to convey this vital message with clarity and impact.

Many leaders assume the benefits of safety measures are self-evident. However, to drive real change, people need to see how these measures personally connect to their lives. As leaders, it's our responsibility to help them make those connections.

These steps will assist you in articulating "The Why."

Start with a Story: Begin with a relatable scenario or case study that highlights both the risks of inaction and the positive outcomes of implementing new safety measures. For instance, share the story of a company that faced dire consequences but transformed after adopting similar safety strategies.

Use Data Strategically: Facts and figures are more than just numbers; they can compellingly support your narrative. For example, illustrate how similar initiatives have statistically reduced accidents, fostering a safer work environment elsewhere.

Relate to Their Experiences: Draw parallels between their daily responsibilities and how these changes specifically protect and benefit them. This shifts perception from abstract rules to personal advantages.

Address Concerns Head-On: Don't overlook potential disruptions. Instead, openly discuss challenges while emphasizing the greater good— closer ties to family through improved safety, enhanced job satisfaction through secure working environments, and the shared responsibility for each other's safety.

Engage Them Actively: Encourage input from your team on how these measures can best be integrated into daily operations. An inclusive approach, where everyone's voice is heard, fosters stronger support than mandates from above.

Acknowledge Contributions: Recognize and celebrate team members who exemplify or advocate for safety, building momentum and inspiring others to follow suit.

Regular Reiteration: Culture and safety improvement is an ongoing commitment, not a one-time effort. Regular communications—newsletters, team meetings, and updates—keep the message fresh and emphasize its importance.

Continuous Feedback: Establish channels for ongoing dialogue. Encouraging feedback loops enables the team to voice concerns, share insights, and influence future modifications based on practical experiences and evolving contexts.

Ultimately, effectively communicating the "why" helps dismantle resistance by aligning safety initiatives with the values and priorities of your workforce. By connecting both emotionally and logically, you can transform initial resistance into lasting advocacy.

I mentioned the importance of engaging the team actively, which must be done collaboratively to achieve optimal results.

Step 4: Make it Collaborative.

Create an Inclusive Environment: Foster a community that values everyone's input. Begin by inviting all team members to participate in a brainstorming session focused on safety changes.

Action: Organize regular "safety huddle" meetings where team members can openly discuss their experiences and suggestions.

Tip: *Ensure these huddles are low-pressure and open-ended to promote genuine dialogue.*

Form Focus Groups: Establish joint owner-worker safety committees tasked with piloting new initiatives and evaluating their effectiveness. Select a diverse group for task forces that includes varying roles, experiences, and seniority levels to ensure a comprehensive perspective.

Tip: *Rotate group members regularly to encourage broader participation and gather fresh insights. To maintain continuity, consider having a core group that remains consistent over time, acting as anchors while others rotate in and out to ensure follow-through and momentum.*

Celebrate Success Together: Publicly acknowledge and celebrate successful initiatives that arise from collaborative efforts.

Tip: *Use newsletters, bulletins, or digital dashboards to keep everyone informed about safety achievements and next steps.*

Maintain Engagement with Ongoing Discovery: Expand your team's understanding and skills related to safety through continuous educational opportunities. Invite experts for workshops or send teams for external safety certifications. This not only enhances skill sets but also demonstrates a commitment to their professional development.

Tip: *Encourage team members to volunteer as trainers or mentors, fostering a peer-to-peer discovery-based environment.*

Implement a feedback system that regularly reviews and responds to suggestions, reinforcing the value of everyone's role in shaping safety practices. Develop partnerships with external safety organizations to conduct regular audits and provide advice, demonstrating the external validation of your efforts.

Creating a collaborative culture to enhance safety goes beyond compliance; it involves harnessing the collective insight and energy of your team. When everyone has a stake in safety, resistance transforms into engagement, and team members become drivers of change rather than followers.

Now that you understand the power of a truly collaborative culture, the next step is to maintain that momentum. Sparking change is one challenge; building something lasting is another. Just as Paul O'Neill faced resistance when he became CEO of Alcoa, the real challenge lies in converting initial pushback into a movement of continuous improvement. In the next chapter, we will explore how to create systems that not only support this progress but also inspire it daily, from the ground up. Real transformation arises not from a one-time effort but from an environment where progress becomes second nature.

CHAPTER 12:
CONTINUOUS IMPROVEMENT

"The road to success is always under construction."
- Arnold Palmer

Picture this scene: a sprawling manufacturing plant, bustling with activity and the rhythmic hum of machinery. Not long ago, this facility diligently ticked off compliance boxes to meet safety standards. Safety was viewed more as a regulatory obligation than a shared value—just another requirement for auditors and insurers. However, over the years, an evolution unfolded—a metamorphosis from struggling to meet compliance to a thriving culture of continuous safety improvement, transforming the plant into a beacon of innovation and excellence.

The driving force behind this revolutionary shift was the leadership at Stellar Performance (a pseudonym for a real organization), who recognized the limitations of a compliance-centric approach to safety. They envisioned a more dynamic, responsive, and inclusive system where safety practices evolved organically from within rather than being dictated from above. Their message resonated with every worker, from front-line operators to top management, fundamentally changing how safety was perceived and practiced.

Stellar initiated this transformation by fostering an environment where every employee felt empowered and responsible for safety. Imagine a place where all workers, regardless of their position, were encouraged to voice their observations and suggestions for improvement without fear of reprimand. The leaders drew inspiration from the concept of Kaizen—a Japanese term meaning "change for the better"—emphasizing small, incremental changes that lead to significant improvements over time.

To implement such a system, Stellar rolled out a structured program where every team began their day with a Safety Huddle. This daily ritual was not just about discussing potential hazards; it served as a forum for sharing personal stories, lessons learned, and innovative ideas that could be applied immediately. Even the smallest ideas shared in these huddles often gained momentum, spreading across teams and evolving into larger initiatives.

For example, a seemingly minor observation by a production line worker about the awkward placement of a machinery control panel led to an ergonomic redesign that dramatically reduced operational errors and physical strain. This not only showcased the value of grassroots input but also reinforced the company's commitment to integrating employee insights into systemic improvements.

The transformation at Stellar was accomplished not through sporadic changes but through the establishment of robust feedback loops. These ensured that insights from the ground level were swiftly communicated to decision-makers, allowing for prompt strategic responses. They adopted digital dashboards where incidents and near-misses were logged in real-time, enabling an agile response to emerging safety issues.

In their Safety Sweeps, Stellar facilitated dynamic sessions where cross-departmental teams addressed recent safety challenges. Ideas clashed and merged, leading to actionable plans and innovative strategies such as reengineering equipment layouts and implementing predictive maintenance models. These sessions highlighted the critical role of collaboration in uncovering risks and driving organizational improvement.

Central to Stellar's success was their strategic investment in education and training. They recognized that fostering a culture of continuous improvement involved not just managing processes but nurturing people's growth and understanding. Every new hire at Stellar underwent an intensive onboarding session that focused not just on safety protocols but also on the philosophy of continuous improvement and the company's cultural initiative.

Employees were provided with ongoing educational opportunities, including safety rotational programs where they exchanged roles within departments to experience and understand diverse safety challenges firsthand. This exchange further strengthened the safety mindset by building empathy and a multidimensional understanding of workplace dynamics.

One compelling narrative from Stellar's transformation involves their logistics division. Faced with a troubling trend of frequent minor injuries during manual material handling, the team utilized daily safety insights meetings to brainstorm solutions. A novel idea emerged: developing smart gloves equipped with sensors that monitored hand positions and cautioned wearers via gentle vibrations when they engaged in potentially harmful movements. This initiative mitigated safety risks and sparked a wave of curiosity and innovation, leading to the creation of more wearable safety devices tailored to various tasks. The success of the smart glove pilot led to a broader rollout across other divisions, significantly reducing strain-related injuries and inspiring the development of additional wearable tech for specialized tasks.

Another illustrative example came from their quality assurance department, which had traditionally operated in silos. By integrating continuous feedback loops and promoting inter-departmental collaboration, the team addressed long-standing safety issues stemming from workflow disconnects. This proactive stance not only reduced errors but also cultivated a cohesive team dynamic underscored by trust and mutual respect.

Ultimately, Stellar's transformation wasn't just technical—it was cultural. By making every employee a contributor to improvement, they built a system that responded dynamically, evolved consistently, and empowered every voice.

As you examine Stellar's exemplary journey, the implications are clear: going beyond compliance involves more than adopting new protocols or tools; it's about instilling a living culture where continuous improvement is the heartbeat of the organization. It acknowledges that every incremental step forward in safety practices can lead to profound, cumulative transformations.

In the next section, we'll explore the tools and techniques used by Stellar and others to maintain this momentum, ensuring that continuous improvement is not just an initiative but a sustained organizational reality.

In the pursuit of exceeding safety compliance, Stellar has mastered the art of leveraging continuous improvement tools and techniques that are practical, measurable, and adaptable. These tools not only empower employees but ensure that improvement is embedded into the daily operations and culture of the organization.

One cornerstone of Stellar's approach to maintaining a belief of continuous improvement is the use of real-time data analytics. In Stellar's main office, a centralized dashboard displays real-time safety data from across the plant. This visibility allows teams to detect trends early, respond to emerging risks, and make data-informed decisions with confidence.

For instance, the company employs advanced dashboard software that aggregates data from various sensors around the plant, tracking everything from equipment vibration levels to employee biometric signals. This information is not just compiled for oversight; it's actively used to anticipate equipment failures or detect unsafe work patterns. Consider the augmented reality (AR) interfaces installed on smart helmets—these project real-time safety data, providing instant situational awareness to their wearers.

Beyond technology, the human factor remains pivotal. Stellar has perfected the art of Kaizen—a Japanese philosophy of continuous improvement through small, ongoing positive changes. During regular Kaizen Events, team members from multiple disciplines collaborate, brainstorm ideas, and implement quick-win projects that enhance safety. These sessions are fertile ground for innovation, as frontline workers engage with engineers and managers, breaking free from hierarchical constraints for creative problem-solving.

During a recent Kaizen event, a cross-functional team tackled the challenge of frequent hand injuries reported on assembly lines. The collective brainstorming led to the development of a custom-made tool grip that minimized injury rates while improving overall task efficiency— a win-win achieved through grassroots involvement.

Stellar maintains a focus on safety through visual management. Large, prominently placed boards display safety progress, incident logs, and active goals, providing teams with an at-a-glance view of collective performance. This visibility ensures that everyone is aligned and engaged with safety objectives.

These visuals are reinforced by daily stand-up meetings, where teams review past outcomes, align on current priorities, and commit to improvement goals. These briefings promote open communication, allowing team members to voice concerns and celebrate successes, fostering a proactive culture with shared ownership.

An illustrative example is the introduction of a "Safety Traffic Light System." At each workstation, a light indicates operational safety levels, turning green to denote compliance, yellow for caution, and red for immediate attention. This simple yet profound system nurtures a dynamic safety environment where real-time status is clearly communicated and acted upon without delay.

Stellar has embraced multimedia training tools as an essential part of their safety strategy. These platforms offer immersive experiences that replicate real-world scenarios, significantly enhancing skills acquisition and retention. For instance, interactive modules allow employees to navigate hazards in a simulated plant environment, reinforcing theoretical knowledge with practical application without exposing them to real hazards.

Furthermore, gamification in training modules has proven especially effective for task mastery and employee engagement. The point system keeps employees motivated while reinforcing everyday safety habits in a fun, approachable way.

In the spirit of continuous improvement, Stellar integrates Lean Six Sigma methodologies to streamline operations while emphasizing safety transformations. Through detailed process mapping and data-driven analysis, unnecessary steps are eliminated, reducing cycle times and potential risks. This synergy between quality and safety creates a robust framework for sustainable operational excellence.

Lean Six Sigma projects have identified previously overlooked redundant procedures that posed risks. By eliminating these redundancies, workflows have been optimized and potential hazards minimized—a testament to the harmony between quality improvement and safety.

For organizations captivated by Stellar's story, the tools and techniques utilized are neither esoteric nor exclusive. They are easily adaptable to any setting willing to embrace change. Whether managing a large plant or a small office, you can start small—leveraging data-driven insights to inform everyday decisions, fostering an environment open to cross-department collaboration, clearly communicating safety objectives, and ensuring consistent skill development among employees.

By cultivating a workplace where continuous improvement becomes second nature, you will not only enhance safety practices but also empower your teams, turning them into advocates for safety in every decision they make. As Stellar illustrates, the journey of continuous improvement is driven by committed leadership and the collective endeavor to achieve safety excellence.

While Stellar's narrative is fictionalized, it reflects real-world trends. Now, let's explore how actual global companies have cultivated similar cultures of safety excellence through unique and varied approaches.

One compelling case study of safety transformation is Siemens, the global technology company, which significantly improved its culture through a comprehensive overhaul starting in the early 2000s.

In 2004, Siemens faced numerous safety challenges across its diverse operations. The company recognized that its traditional compliance-focused approach was inadequate for addressing the evolving needs for workplace safety globally. In response, Siemens initiated a strategic program called "Zero Harm Culture."

The "Zero Harm Culture" initiative aimed to make safety an intrinsic part of every employee's daily activities. Siemens emphasized the importance of leadership commitment at all levels. Executives and managers were expected to lead by example, integrating safety discussions into all operations and making it a key component of performance evaluations.

A pivotal element of Siemens' strategy was engaging employees through innovative training and awareness programs. The company developed immersive training sessions that addressed practical safety issues relevant to specific roles and locations. This targeted approach tailored safety education, making it more relatable and impactful.

Siemens also fostered continuous improvement by encouraging employees to contribute ideas for safety enhancements. By incentivizing safety innovations and maintaining an open feedback loop, Siemens created shared responsibility and engagement.

To support these initiatives, Siemens invested in state-of-the-art safety technologies and data analytics. These tools enabled real-time monitoring of safety processes and highlighted potential risks before they escalated into incidents.

The success of Siemens' safety transformation is evident in measurable outcomes. The company achieved a significant reduction in its Lost Time Injury Frequency Rate (LTIFR), a common industry metric for workplace safety. From 2004 to 2014, Siemens reported a reduction in LTIFR of over 60%. This achievement stemmed from the holistic integration of safety into their business operations, reinforcing that safety is a critical component of business excellence.

Siemens' commitment to safety has been recognized through numerous industry awards, highlighting its leadership in proactive safety management. The company's approach has set a benchmark for other global organizations seeking comprehensive safety solutions that extend beyond compliance.

The *zero-harm* philosophy aims to eliminate all workplace injuries but often faces criticism for potentially encouraging underreporting and hindering learning from mistakes. However, when paired with psychological safety and honest dialogue, this approach can still serve as an aspirational goal. It's most effective when it inspires vigilance and proactive safety practices rather than suppressing truth. By combining the ideals of "zero harm" with a supportive culture, organizations can balance ambition with the practical realities of human error and risk management.

At the heart of modern safety lies a philosophical divide: Should we pursue "Zero Harm," eliminating every possible incident, or focus on creating resilient systems that expect and learn from human error? Siemens exemplifies the Zero Harm philosophy, setting a global standard in proactive safety management by striving for incident-free environments.

Conversely, Cintas Corporation embraces learning, viewing safety as an evolving landscape where continuous learning and adaptability drive long-term success. This approach acknowledges that safety must accommodate human fallibility and incorporates ongoing improvement as a core component.

Impactful Insights:

- Siemens focuses on entirely eliminating risks, aspiring toward perfection through systematic controls.
- Cintas emphasizes learning from mistakes and fostering open communication and adaptability, recognizing that human error is part of the process.

Both Siemens and Cintas present compelling models: one aspires toward perfection while the other embraces human fallibility. The right choice depends on your context, but both demonstrate that intentional culture-building yields powerful, measurable results.

Cintas analyzed incidents to uncover root causes, emphasizing systems and processes rather than assigning blame.

By encouraging open incident reporting without fear of punishment, Cintas gained valuable insights to enhance safety practices.

The company prioritizes improving systems and processes, acknowledging the inevitability of human error and the importance of resilience. Initiatives focus on empowering employees to recognize and mitigate hazards, promoting mindfulness and situational awareness.

Over time, Cintas achieved significant reductions in workplace incidents, driven by improved processes and employee engagement. Employees felt more engaged and empowered to contribute to safety improvements, fostering a proactive work environment.

Philosophical differences between the two approaches are evident. The zero-harm philosophy raises concerns about underreporting, as workers may avoid reporting incidents to maintain the "zero harm" status. Strict adherence can create fear, stifling openness and innovation.

Cintas and other organizations believe in the advantages of intentional learning, emphasizing honest reporting and understanding rather than fear of repercussions. Focusing on learning from incidents encourages adaptability and ongoing improvement.

These differing philosophies highlight a fundamental debate in safety management. While zero harm seeks to eliminate all incidents, a learning culture recognizes the complexities of human behavior and the inevitability of mistakes, promoting resilience and systemic improvement. Cintas Corporation's approach exemplifies the potential benefits of fostering an environment that prioritizes growth and safety evolution.

CHAPTER 13:
THE BIG DEBATE

"To improve is to change; to be perfect is to change often."
– Winston Churchill

A debate unfolds as safety is placed under scrutiny. Imagine a bright conference room bustling with energy, where consultants from various sectors passionately discuss the merits of behavior-based safety (BBS) versus operational learning (Human and Organizational Performance, or HOP). The room buzzes with animated dialogue, each expert attempting to capture the essence of their preferred methodology. Proponents of behavior-based safety emphasize its proven track record in altering unsafe behaviors through observation and feedback. In contrast, supporters of operational learning argue that understanding organizational systems and human factors is key to preventing unsafe scenarios before they occur.

This debate isn't just academic; it reflects the real-world decisions organizations face when building safer environments. Both philosophies are integral to reducing workplace injuries, and finding harmony between them can lead to a robust culture where preventive practices and responsive adaptations go hand in hand.

I've seen consultants casually dismiss behavior-based safety (BBS), labeling it as outdated, ineffective, or even harmful, without taking the time to understand its intent or evolution. Yes, BBS has its flaws—every method does. However, when implemented thoughtfully—empowering workers rather than blaming them—BBS can facilitate crucial conversations that lead to real change. It can enlighten leaders about the realities of work and spark improvements that save lives. Completely dismissing it hinders safety progress and strips organizations of a valuable tool that, when refined, could contribute to their growth.

To those quick to dismiss: critiquing from the sidelines is easy. True leadership involves rolling up your sleeves, asking better questions, and assisting teams in improving what they already have. If you genuinely care about safety, help organizations evolve—don't just tear down what they've built or aspire to create. They need builders, not cynics. Be one.

Some consultants caution against operational learning, suggesting it could damage culture. However, dismissing Human and Organizational Performance (HOP) overlooks its potential to deepen understanding and reduce harm. Once a solid foundation is established, HOP doesn't weaken your system; it elevates it. Safety is more than policy; it's a mindset of continuous learning.

To the consultants and leaders giving that advice: I urge you to reconsider your impact. When you instill fear instead of confidence, when you defend the status quo and your narrative rather than challenge it, you aren't helping organizations; you're preventing them from saving lives. If we are truly here to serve and enhance workplace safety, we must tell the truth, even when it's messy. Real leadership means having the courage to guide organizations through discomfort, not around it.

Both BBS and HOP contribute essential elements to the safety conversation—one grounded in observable behavior, the other in systems thinking. Together, they provide a more comprehensive view of how to keep people safe, creating a balanced framework for safety excellence, continuous improvement, and empowerment at all levels.

In essence, behavior-based safety shouldn't simply focus on fixing problems as they arise; it should foster an atmosphere where everyone actively prevents them, especially when implemented with purpose. To illustrate the power of this approach, let's examine a real-world example: an energy company that strategically adopted a behavior-based safety program to transform its entire safety performance.

BBS is a proactive strategy that encourages employees to identify and correct unsafe behaviors in the workplace. It transcends from adhering to regulations, to aiming to cultivate a belief that promotes employee involvement and ownership. A compelling example of BBS success is the story of an energy company that undertook this transformative journey.

The organization faced significant challenges in maintaining safety due to the inherently risky nature of the oil and gas industry. Leadership recognized that traditional safety measures, primarily focused on equipment and compliance, could not achieve the desired reduction in workplace accidents. Acknowledging the limitations of compliance alone, the company embraced a behavior-based approach that emphasized peer observations, feedback, and ownership.

The initiative commenced with a comprehensive baseline assessment to understand existing safety behaviors and overall culture. This stage involved detailed observations, interviews, and surveys targeting various staff levels to identify common unsafe behaviors, their root causes, and barriers to safe practices.

Following the initial assessment, the energy company launched a meticulously planned BBS program. The cornerstone of their strategy was engaging employees at all levels in the safety process. Training sessions educated employees on the importance of behavior in safety, emphasizing observation techniques and feedback mechanisms. Workers learned to conduct peer-to-peer observations, identifying both safe and unsafe behaviors, and how to deliver constructive feedback.

A vital component of the BBS program was the formation of safety committees comprising volunteers from different departments. These committees analyzed observation data, identified trends, and developed targeted interventions. This grassroots involvement ensured that employees felt ownership of the safety process rather than perceiving it as a top-down directive.

Moreover, the energy company heavily invested in its communication strategy to support the BBS initiative. The organization promoted open communication, allowing employees to discuss safety concerns without fear of reprisal. This transparency was essential for dismantling mistrust and encouraging honest reporting of potential hazards.

The results of the BBS program were both tangible and significant. Leaders reported a substantial drop in injury incidents. Within a few years of implementing BBS, the company observed a 40% reduction in Total Recordable Incident Rate (TRIR). Additionally, near-miss reporting increased, indicating improved awareness and a more vigilant workforce in identifying risks before they could lead to harm.

Beyond reducing injuries, there was a marked improvement in overall safety performance. Employees felt more responsible for their actions and actively engaged in safety initiatives. The empowerment of individuals to take ownership of safety facilitated a shift from compliance-based to trust-based safety leadership.

The transition to a behavior-based safety initiative yielded benefits beyond safety improvements. It fostered a collaborative working environment, enhanced communication, increased morale, and built trust between management and the workforce. This comprehensive transformation underscored the impact of BBS on both operational performance and workplace culture.

This case exemplifies how companies can move beyond traditional compliance-oriented safety practices to create participative safety grounded in behavioral principles. Through strategic planning, engagement, and communication, BBS can drive safety excellence while fostering a more cohesive and motivated workforce.

While the energy company showcased the transformative power of behavior-based safety, operational learning has demonstrated equal promise in entirely different environments. A standout example comes from the healthcare industry, where lives are at stake daily. Enter Intermountain Healthcare: a compelling illustration of how operational learning and a just culture can turn bold ideas into everyday reality. Based in Utah, Intermountain Healthcare is a non-profit health system with an innovative approach that leverages operational learning principles and just culture. This case study reveals how focusing on people and processes fosters an environment of trust and enhances overall outcomes.

Intermountain Healthcare's journey began with recognition of the traditional approach's limitations, where compliance often overshadowed meaningful patient outcomes. Leadership understood that a shift from a compliance-focused to a performance-oriented culture was vital. They aimed to cultivate a work environment rooted in trust and continuous learning, yielding transformative results in patient care and operational efficiency.

Key to Intermountain's strategy was the implementation of Clinical Program Leadership, a model encouraging teamwork and collaboration among physicians, nurses, and administrators. This strategy empowered medical staff by involving them directly in decision-making processes related to patient care protocols. By valuing the insights and expertise of frontline healthcare workers, Intermountain harnessed a wealth of knowledge that compliance-driven cultures often stifle.

An important aspect of this transformation was the organization's commitment to transparency and data-driven decision-making. Intermountain developed standardized processes for consistent evaluation of outcomes across different healthcare facilities. This transparency fostered an atmoshere where staff felt comfortable discussing failures openly, viewing them as opportunities for learning rather than points of blame.

For example, Intermountain's approach to infection control epitomized this shift. Instead of enforcing rigid compliance-based procedures, Intermountain encouraged teams to evaluate the root causes of failures and collaborate on developing solutions. This led to a significant reduction in hospital-acquired infections, a critical measure of patient safety.

Moreover, leadership at Intermountain played a crucial role in cultivating trust. They prioritized listening and responding to healthcare workers' needs, understanding that trust is built when employees feel heard and valued. This was complemented by investments in continuous learning opportunities, enabling staff to acquire new skills and knowledge, thus reinforcing a cycle of both professional and organizational growth.

The impact of Intermountain Healthcare's transformation was profound. They achieved significant improvements in patient care and safety while also enhancing employee satisfaction and retention rates. The organization's emphasis on operational learning led to reduced costs and increased value for patients, demonstrating that a trust-based principle yields benefits beyond compliance.

The principles Intermountain implemented resonate universally. By prioritizing human potential and organizational performance, they transcended traditional compliance, setting a new standard in the healthcare industry. Their experience illustrates that when organizations focus on trust and learning, transformative outcomes follow. Such a culture not only advances business objectives but also cultivates a more humane and effective workplace.

Pause here—this moment matters. Real leadership isn't about rushing ahead; it's about mastering the essentials with care. If something stirs you, don't rush past it. Sit with it. Let it change how you lead.

When you internalize these essentials, real change isn't just possible—it becomes inevitable. That's exactly what we're witnessing in organizations leading the way. In the pursuit of exemplary safety standards and transformative business results, organizations increasingly recognize the value of Human and Organizational Performance (HOP) as a pivotal framework. A compelling example is WestRock, a leading provider of packaging solutions, which successfully leveraged HOP principles to instigate a cultural shift that enhanced trust and performance across the board.

WestRock, operating over 300 facilities globally with a workforce exceeding 50,000, understood the critical need to embed safety into its organizational fabric. The challenge lay in moving beyond compliance-based safety measures to foster a workplace rooted in trust and continuous learning.

WestRock's journey began with a shift in mindset—from placing individual blame for incidents to addressing the deeper systemic issues that contribute to errors. This involved a strategic initiative to implement

HOP, emphasizing five fundamentals: learning, variability, adaptability, leadership commitment, and accountability.

The leadership at WestRock recognized that trust within teams is essential for effective learning and improvement. They initiated a series of workshops and training sessions aimed at educating leaders and workers about HOP principles. This outreach conveyed a clear message: safety is not just about procedural compliance but a core value.

As part of embracing HOP, WestRock encouraged open dialogue, allowing employees to voice concerns and share experiences without fear of retribution. This transparency was crucial in identifying potential risks and areas for improvement. WestRock also viewed human error as a symptom rather than a cause, directing efforts toward enhancing systems and processes to better serve the workforce.

One significant shift was the leadership's decision to model trust and integrity. They adopted a conditional approach to safety metrics, focusing on understanding the "why" behind the numbers rather than simply achieving targets. This approach emphasizes context and conditions, such as operational systems and workplace pressures, creating a comprehensive picture that helps organizations address root causes and enhance safety outcomes.

WestRock implemented feedback loops, enabling rapid communication of lessons learned and corrective actions. This not only improved safety outcomes but also fostered an environment where workers felt valued and heard—crucial elements in building trust.

The results of these initiatives were tangible. WestRock experienced marked improvements in safety performance, evidenced by reduced incident rates and enhanced operational efficiency. Staff morale and engagement improved as the organizational culture shifted from defensive compliance to proactive, trust-driven learning.

In summary, WestRock effectively utilized HOP to transform its organizational culture. By promoting learning, embracing variability, and fostering an environment of trust, the company achieved superior safety and business outcomes. This case underscores the power of trust as an enabler of not just safety excellence but holistic organizational success.

What kind of culture are you really building? It doesn't start with programs—it starts with purpose. No single method holds the answer. The real power lies in combining tools, guided by humility and the belief that every insight could be the one that protects someone you care about. Because that's where it begins—not with programs or systems, but with a shared vision of who we want to be together.

There are countless tools and mindsets available: compliance programs, EHS management systems, Behavior-Based Safety, Old View, New View, Safety I, Safety II, Operational Learning, Human Factors, and Human and Organizational Performance. While the names, frameworks, and mindsets may differ, they all aim to achieve the same goal: to help us protect what matters most—*our people.*

It's not about choosing one over the other or chasing the latest trend. It's about embracing anything that brings us closer to a culture where trust is real, ownership is shared, and safety isn't just a rule—it's a value lived out loud. It's about adopting a mindset that says: We are here to learn. We are here to understand everything we can—every day—because every insight we gain could be the one that keeps someone safe.

Never forget: **People are the silver bullet**. Listening to those doing the work will certainly lead to better outcomes.

Remember, the priority is simple: People First. Safety Always. Once that mental model is planted, it's time to look inward. What's guiding your decisions today? As you reflect, consider personal leadership and continuous learning as keys to transformation. In the next section, we'll examine how self-awareness and adaptability in leadership pave the way for overcoming resistance and fostering trust.

Earlier in the chapter, we explored how some organizations have truly transformed their safety outcomes—and the results were powerful. Now, take a moment to reflect on your own strategy. Are you relying on just one mindset or method?

Think about it like building a house. You wouldn't show up with just a hammer and expect to finish the job, right? It takes a whole toolkit—each tool playing a different, essential role. So why would building a strong culture—one rooted in trust, collaboration, and shared ownership—be any different?

Let's pause for a moment and really dig into the essence of accountability. Trust, engagement, and responsibility—when woven together—will naturally lead to shared ownership through accountability. But what does accountability truly mean to you? Is it accurately reflected in your expectations, or do those around you play a guessing game with the standards you hold internally? Consider this deeply as we dive into the next chapter on accountability. Reflect on how you communicate and enforce accountability in your leadership. Are your expectations crystal clear? Or unknowingly hidden in your mind, waiting to be discovered? These profound questions invite us to re-evaluate and refine our approach to truly lead with integrity and clarity.

CHAPTER 14:
ACCOUNTABILITY

"On good teams coaches hold players accountable, on great teams players hold players accountable"
– Joe Dumars

Let's start this chapter with a cautionary tale that highlights the hazards of unclear accountability. In a fast-paced manufacturing plant, a seemingly ordinary day descended into chaos when a forklift collided with a shelving unit, causing it to collapse and materials to fall to the concrete floor. The loud noise startled everyone, sending waves of confusion through the workforce. The incident injured a worker and disrupted operations, revealing a critical flaw in the organization's system: a lack of accountability.

As the dust settled, it became clear that the event was not isolated but symptomatic of a deeper issue. Nobody knew who was accountable for ensuring the forklift's maintenance or the operator's training. Each department assumed the other was overseeing these aspects, leaving glaring gaps in safety protocols unchecked.

This diffusion of responsibility mirrors the historical "Tragedy of the Commons," seen vividly in 19th-century London. There, common land overused by individual herders acting in self-interest eventually rendered the land barren, underscoring the pitfalls of unregulated communal resources.

Much like the commons in London, where shared ownership led to resource depletion due to a lack of individual accountability, the manufacturing plant suffered from everyone assuming someone else was responsible.

Recognizing this issue, the plant's leadership embarked on a transformation. They implemented a structured accountability framework where each employee clearly understood their roles in safety. By assigning personal responsibility and fostering ownership and proactive communication, they significantly improved safety, boosted morale, and increased operational efficiency.

Accountability is the cornerstone of a proactive culture, ensuring clarity, ownership, and effective communication among all workplace participants.

True accountability empowers rather than isolates. It's about fostering a culture where each person understands their responsibilities, feels ownership over safety protocols, and communicates effectively to prevent incidents before they happen. This proactive stance transforms safety from a set of rules into a shared mindset.

When everyone understands their specific roles, confusion dissipates, and safety evolves from a policy into practice. Clarity acts as an invisible guide, transforming well-intentioned procedures into purposeful actions. Without it, even the most robust safety plans can descend into chaos and uncertainty.

Even in fictional settings like *Saving Private Ryan*, the importance of role clarity is powerfully illustrated. Captain Miller's precise delegation—akin to effective leadership in any high-stakes environment—ensures his team operates with unity and purpose. This cinematic example highlights the necessity of role clarity for success, whether in battle or on the shop floor.

Before proceeding, take a moment to consider: how clearly are roles and expectations defined in your organization?

Consider a new safety protocol for chemical handling at a manufacturing plant. The directive vaguely states, "Handle all chemicals with care and use appropriate protective gear." Without specifics—such as which chemicals or what gear—employees are left guessing. This ambiguity dilutes responsibility, reducing a straightforward directive to a guessing game. The lack of clarity undermines safety and engagement, leaving room for interpretation that could result in over-caution, inefficiencies, or, worse, underestimating hazards. This scenario emphasizes that clear directives strengthen both safety culture and ownership, ensuring everyone understands their role and the expectations involved.

This confusion resembles a captain navigating a ship without clear maps—each crew member might interpret the course differently, creating a scatter of paths instead of a united front. Clarity is the map that ensures everyone steers in the right direction, avoiding collisions and achieving safety excellence without detours.

Imagine you're not just a passenger on the ship, but an integral part of the crew. The map may offer guidance, yet your vigilance and commitment keep the vessel on course. When ownership is embraced, safety becomes a shared journey across all levels of the organization.

Shared ownership transforms safety into a personal commitment instead of a box-check exercise. When employees take ownership, everything shifts. They adhere to protocols, report hazards, and advocate for improvements. Ownership flourishes when workers participate in developing safety policies, feel empowered to voice concerns, and are recognized for their contributions to a safe work environment.

In the competitive world of business, the concept of "shared ownership" has emerged as a vital factor in fostering an environment that evolves into genuine commitment. This concept is vividly illustrated by the case of Morning Star, a tomato processing company that has thrived by implementing a unique organizational structure grounded in shared ownership and self-management.

Morning Star exemplifies how an organization can harness the power of shared ownership. Founded by Chris Rufer in 1970, the company revolutionized the approach by eliminating traditional hierarchical management roles. Instead, Morning Star operates on the principle of self-management, granting every employee the autonomy to make decisions and take ownership of their roles and responsibilities.

This shift to a decentralized model has had profound implications for safety and overall performance. Without traditional managerial oversight, employees at Morning Star are empowered to identify safety hazards, propose solutions, and implement measures to mitigate risks. By moving beyond compliance to personal commitment, the company has witnessed remarkable improvements in safety outcomes.

The key to this transformation is Morning Star's Colleague Letter of Understanding (CLOU), a vital instrument embodying shared ownership. Every employee crafts their CLOU, detailing their responsibilities, performance metrics, and mission objectives, all aligned with the company's overarching goals. This document enhances accountability and fosters a deep sense of ownership, as employees have a direct role in shaping their responsibilities.

The impact on safety is significant. Aware that their peers rely on them to maintain a safe workplace, employees are more motivated to adhere to safety protocols and report potential hazards. This proactive culture nurtures a continuous improvement mindset. Employees constantly seek ways to enhance their processes, promoting an evolving safety culture.

A tangible manifestation of this culture can be seen in Morning Star's exceptional safety record. Despite the inherent dangers of the food processing industry, the company boasts accident rates significantly lower than the industry average. This success largely stems from the employee-driven nature of safety practices. Employees are motivated not by mandates from above, but by their intrinsic desire to contribute to a safe workplace.

Moreover, shared ownership at Morning Star fosters open communication. Employees feel empowered to voice concerns without fear of repercussions. This open dialogue is crucial for proactively addressing safety issues and turning potential threats into opportunities for innovation and growth. With everyone invested in the company's success, collective problem-solving thrives.

The notion of shared ownership extends beyond safety. It permeates all facets of Morning Star's operations, driving the company to unparalleled productivity and profitability. By investing in its workforce and embracing a culture of trust and autonomy, Morning Star has cultivated not only a safe work environment but also a thriving business.

Morning Star's model has been profiled in publications like Harvard Business Review and featured in workplace innovation studies for its radical decentralization and results. It underscores the transformative power that shared ownership can have within an organization. By transitioning from compliance to genuine commitment, companies can inspire their employees to engage wholeheartedly, resulting in enhanced safety, innovation, and competitive advantage.

As you reflect on Morning Star's approach, ask yourself: as a leader, are you enforcing accountability—or cultivating it? True accountability doesn't arise from pressure; it flourishes in environments where people feel ownership, purpose, and the freedom to speak up. This growth begins with communication. It's through open, honest dialogue that shared missions transform into meaningful actions.

This week, examine how accountability manifests in your team. Are conversations about safety and responsibility top-down mandates, or do they encourage collaboration and ownership?

Start one conversation today that opens the door for feedback, mutual respect, and shared commitment. You might be surprised at how far a simple, sincere dialogue can go in strengthening your culture of accountability.

Communication is the glue binding responsibility and action. By fostering open, regular dialogue about safety issues and expectations, organizations create a feedback loop that identifies potential threats before they lead to accidents. This communication must flow in all directions—upward, downward, and laterally—to be most effective.

Leaders must exemplify accountability and prioritize safety. Their actions set a standard for the entire organization, demonstrating that safety isn't a siloed policy but a core value that is integrated into the overall business. Leaders need to model what they expect. Accountability starts at the top. If leaders want their teams to take ownership, they must first demonstrate what that looks like in action. It's insufficient to discuss accountability in meetings or include it in performance reviews—teams observe how leaders respond under pressure, admit mistakes, and consistently follow through on their commitments.

This principle hit me with full force one Good Friday morning when I was jolted awake by the shrill ring of the phone. On the line was a familiar voice—a trusted colleague. It was the Plant Manager from one of our facilities. I answered with a cheerful, "Good morning," only to be met with the unexpected:

"Hey... we burned down the tank farm."

I quickly assured him I'd catch the next available flight to help. A dear colleague of mine joined me on this critical trip, and together we headed out to support the plant. Over Easter weekend, we worked tirelessly with the team to uncover what had caused the fire.

By Monday, Human Resources was at our door, pressing us for answers being demanded by higher leadership:

"So, who is it going to be? The 'Leader' wants to know who needs to be fired—the Plant Manager or the Production Manager?"

With a steady voice, I replied, "We are in the middle of an investigation to ensure we take the right corrective actions and prevent this from happening again at any of our facilities."

As we dug deeper, piecing together the circumstances of the incident, one glaring truth emerged: the 'Leader' had instructed the plant personnel to move forward without conducting a proper risk assessment. They had followed his orders, which inadvertently contributed to the blaze. Our final report made it clear—the plant team had been executing his directives.

After that day, I couldn't shake the feeling that I had a target painted on my back. Still, I was at peace with that, knowing we were committed to uncovering the full context of what had happened. I'm confident that today, the plant team would respond differently, but I also understand the immense pressure they were under at the time. The 'Leader,' however, never took any responsibility.

That incident changed the way I approach everything. It taught me the importance of seeking context—of focusing on what led to events rather than the events themselves. I've learned that asking curious questions often reveals more than I ever imagined. Experiences like these underscore the critical role of leadership in shaping an organization's culture, especially when it comes to accountability.

A leader models accountability by:

- Owning their mistakes publicly. When something goes wrong, a strong leader doesn't point fingers—they reflect, acknowledge their role, and discuss how they plan to improve. This vulnerability doesn't diminish respect; it builds trust, showing the team that accountability is about growth, not blame.
- Following through consistently. Whether it's attending meetings on time, delivering on promises, or addressing difficult conversations, consistency is key. Leaders who honor their word— even in small matters—signal that commitments matter, and that others are expected to do the same.
- Providing and receiving feedback openly. Leaders who seek feedback and act on it create a culture where feedback is safe and welcome. They don't just critique—they invite critique. This demonstrates that everyone, regardless of title, is responsible for improvement.
- Creating an atmosphere for others to own. Micromanagement undermines accountability. A leader who empowers their team to make decisions, learn from outcomes, and lead initiatives communicates trust. They step back not because they don't care, but because they believe in their people.

- Recognizing accountable behavior. Real positive reinforcement is key to building an ownership culture. When someone takes responsibility, admits a mistake, or goes above and beyond to correct an issue, acknowledge it. Recognition reinforces the right behaviors and helps shape the team's norms around ownership.

When leaders consistently model accountability, they establish a clear standard that helps teams understand expectations and inspires them to take ownership and do the right thing. Accountability cannot be delegated; it must be demonstrated. Teams take their cues from leadership, and when leaders model accountability, they set a standard that clarifies expectations.

More importantly, this approach inspires a mindset shift: people begin to take ownership not out of obligation, but out of desire. They view accountability not as a burden, but as a shared commitment to excellence and integrity. Over time, this example fosters a culture where doing the right thing becomes the norm rather than the exception.

However, accountability is not just about assigning responsibility; it's about cultivating a culture that distinguishes between blame and ownership. This leads us to the concept of Just Culture, which provides a framework for learning from mistakes without fear.

Before we continue, consider this: are you fostering true accountability, or shifting blame? While they may appear similar, their effects are vastly different. Blame isolates, whereas accountability empowers. Understanding this distinction is crucial for building a culture that supports both safety and growth, which is where the concept of *Just Culture* comes into play.

Exploring the difference between blame and accountability is vital for creating a culture that prioritizes safety and growth over punishment. A compelling way to illustrate this is through the paradigm of Just Culture, which examines the nuances of blame versus accountability by focusing on systemic improvement rather than individual fault.

The term "Just Culture" emerged in the 1990s, championed by safety experts like David Marx. Just Culture acknowledges human fallibility and recognizes that errors are inevitable aspects of human activity. Instead of solely punishing individuals for mistakes, it emphasizes understanding the broader context, including organizational policies, procedures, and cultures that contribute to errors.

Consider a major airline that faced multiple safety incidents attributed to pilot errors. Initially, the company disciplined the pilots involved, believing punishment would deter future mistakes. However, this approach led to low morale and a culture of fear, where pilots were reluctant to report minor errors or near-misses, resulting in missed opportunities for organizational learning.

Recognizing the unsustainability of this culture, the airline adopted a Just Culture framework. They began conducting thorough investigations not only to identify errors but also to understand the underlying systems and processes contributing to those errors. They discovered that many incidents stemmed not from individual negligence but from inadequate training, outdated manuals, and systemic communication failures.

Transitioning to a Just Culture required a significant mindset shift. The airline's leadership publicly committed to transparency, pledging that honest reporting would not result in punitive actions unless there was evidence of reckless behavior. This cultivation of trust encouraged employees to report errors, enabling the airline to address systemic issues proactively.

A critical element of Just Culture is differentiating between culpable and non-culpable behavior. Not all mistakes warrant the same response; understanding the reasons behind an error is essential. Culpable actions, such as intentional rule-breaking, require a disciplinary approach. However, most errors result from slips, lapses, and honest mistakes that call for systemic solutions rather than punishment.

For instance, in the airline's revised approach, when a pilot inadvertently input incorrect data into the flight management system due to an ambiguous procedure, they examined the procedure itself rather than blaming the pilot. This led to a clearer procedure and additional training for all pilots, demonstrating accountability through constructive changes.

Moreover, the Just Culture framework highlights the essential role leaders play in modeling accountability. Leaders must be open to scrutinizing organizational policies and practices, ensuring they facilitate safety rather than hinder it. Communication from leadership should emphasize learning and improvement, aligning with the cultural shift from blame to accountability.

This transformation within the airline not only improved safety metrics but also enhanced employee engagement and trust. Employees felt supported and valued, knowing their insights contributed to creating safer operational environments. This case exemplifies how accountability encompasses both individual and organizational responsibilities, ensuring actions align with broader safety objectives.

The distinction between blame and accountability is subtle yet profound. Blame isolates individuals, eroding trust and stifling open communication, whereas accountability fosters a culture of continuous learning and systemic improvement. It encourages leaders to adopt a holistic view, recognizing that mistakes often arise from multiple interconnected factors rather than a single point of failure. This shift in perspective—from isolating blame to embracing accountability—comes to life through real-world examples.

Let's return to the forklift incident. Re-examining it through the lens of learning rather than blame reveals how leadership set the tone for change. Instead of reacting with immediate judgment when a driver accidentally struck a shelving unit, leaders approached the incident with curiosity and a focus on improvement. By uncovering potential systemic weaknesses rather than singling out the driver, they reinforced a culture of continuous learning.

Now, consider initiating one genuine conversation today—an exchange that invites feedback, ownership, and collaboration. You'll be amazed at how a single dialogue can shape a culture where accountability and progress thrive. As we move into the next chapter, understanding the subtle habits and mindsets that affect cultural change will equip you to protect and enhance the environment you're cultivating. What steps will you take to foster a space where innovation and safety coexist seamlessly? It's time to act and make a difference.

True accountability doesn't wait for disaster; it's built every day through consistent action, open dialogue, and shared purpose. When teams see leaders owning their words and their work, they rise to do the same. That's how cultures change—from the inside out.

It's time to face the barriers head-on and uncover the lurking culture killers. I'm confident that each of you has witnessed at least one in action. So, let's roll up our sleeves and tackle them together—dig in to expose, understand, and dismantle the obstacles that may be hindering progress.

CHAPTER 15:
CULTURE KILLERS

"Culture eats strategy for breakfast."
– Peter Drucker

Despite its bright posters promoting teamwork, XYZ Corporation was mired in mistrust and finger-pointing. Decisions were made behind closed doors, innovative ideas were routinely dismissed, and the culture slowly suffocated. Despite their efforts, something crucial was missing: authenticity. Employees whispered about decisions made in secrecy, while managers brushed off innovative suggestions with a curt, "We've always done it this way." The once vibrant workplace had been choked by a toxic atmosphere, making it clear that change was necessary.

This situation is not isolated; many organizations, despite their best intentions, grapple with deep-seated cultural issues that stifle progress and erode trust. These hidden pitfalls, or 'culture killers,' are often woven into the very fabric of an organization's operations, quietly undermining efforts to create a positive and productive environment.

Understanding and addressing the hidden habits, decisions, and mindsets that constitute 'culture killers' is essential for nurturing a workplace where trust, ownership, and continuous improvement thrive.

At Morning Star, a tomato processing company, every employee crafts their own Colleague Letter of Understanding, aligning responsibility with autonomy. It's a model of accountability without hierarchy—and it works.

In this chapter, we will dissect the subtle yet destructive forces that haunt workplaces, slowly poisoning the roots of trust and collaboration. Our journey will cover common culture killers that plague organizational environments, their detrimental impacts, and the strategies leaders can employ to excise these poisons, transforming their workplaces into sanctuaries of innovation and mutual respect.

Organizations that cling to outdated practices stifle creativity. Resistance to exploring new methods or ideas breeds an environment where innovation is rarely realized. It's not uncommon for organizations to invest time and resources in hiring subject matter experts—individuals with deep knowledge and fresh perspectives—only to consistently dismiss the very ideas they were brought in to offer. Often, new suggestions are met with familiar responses like, "We tried that before," or "That won't work here."

This raises an important question: Are we truly open to new thinking, or are we simply reinforcing what's comfortable and familiar? If we're unwilling to listen to new voices and explore different approaches, we risk stagnation—regardless of how talented the individuals we hire may be.

Take a moment to reflect: Is your organization creating space for new thinking to take root? As a leader, are you fostering a culture that welcomes possibility, or one that quietly resists it? Why did you feel the need to recruit a subject matter expert in the first place?

Consider this—if you're hiring experts, it's because you recognize your team has knowledge gaps. So why bring them in only to silence their voices? Once they're on board, how often are their insights given room to grow? This brings us to a deeper issue—one that sits at the core of many organizations.

At the heart of many organizations lies a critical flaw that stifles great ideas and suffocates innovation: resistance to change. This resistance isn't just a mindset; it's often embedded in the structure itself, rooted in an overreliance on titles and hierarchical systems. It manifests in organizations that prioritize rank over expertise, turning a deaf ear to those with practical knowledge. Paradoxically, leaders may possess the least experience in areas crucial for innovation.

In traditional structures, decision-making is frequently reserved for those with the highest ranks, regardless of their understanding of the issue at hand. This model assumes that leadership inherently possesses superior knowledge across all topics—a dangerous assumption that overlooks valuable insights from those on the frontlines. Often, the best ideas come from individuals who have hands-on experience with processes and challenges. Yet, their contributions are sidelined simply because they lack a leadership title. This reliance on hierarchy creates an echo chamber effect, where only a few voices are heard, inadvertently suppressing outside-the-box thinking.

The need for leaders to seek the best solutions, rather than assuming they must have all the answers, is a cultural shift many organizations fail to make. Leadership does not equate to omniscience. Effective leaders recognize their role as facilitators of innovation rather than sole problem-solvers. They understand that the wealth of experience often lies with those who have encountered challenges directly and that their role includes empowering these individuals to share insights and drive change.

Overcoming this ingrained resistance to change requires a cultural transformation where collaboration and openness become core values.

Instead of clinging to the past, organizations must cultivate an environment that celebrates diverse thought and encourages contributions from all levels. Leaders should be trained to ask questions rather than provide directives. Practices such as open forums, cross-functional teams, and regular feedback sessions can dismantle silos, fostering a sense that everyone has a stake in collective success.

The transformation begins with a shift in mindset, recognizing that leadership is as much about listening and enabling as it is about guiding and making decisions. When leaders prioritize input over titles, they tap into a rich vein of untapped potential, setting the stage for a culture of continuous improvement and innovation. Embracing and anticipating change requires courage, both to challenge the status quo and to trust that the best ideas may come from those without traditional credentials or authority. This mindset fosters innovation and trust. When everyone feels empowered to speak up, it strengthens accountability and helps prevent small issues from becoming larger problems.

Transparency is crucial for building trust. When people understand what's happening and the reasons behind decisions, they feel included and empowered. This openness eliminates suspicion and promotes a sense of ownership.

Transparent communication and operations foster trust by ensuring that everyone—from executives to entry-level employees—has access to the information necessary to perform their roles effectively. It empowers individuals by providing the knowledge needed to make informed decisions, fostering a sense of inclusion and ownership. This openness mitigates fears of hidden agendas and reduces the likelihood of misinformation, thereby strengthening internal bonds.

An organization that values transparency benefits from cultural cohesion—a state where every employee feels aligned with the company's vision and values. The practice of openly sharing information and decisions encourages a culture of honesty and openness, qualities reflected in daily interactions between employees and management. Such transparency discourages gossip and false narratives, championing a culture where issues are addressed directly rather than whispered in corridors.

When operations and decisions are visible, accountability naturally follows. Employees understand their roles within the larger framework and can see how their contributions impact organizational goals. Transparency highlights areas requiring improvement and showcases successes, motivating teams through recognition while providing clear avenues for support and development.

A transparent environment also serves as fertile ground for innovation. When information flows freely, ideas can be cross-pollinated without friction, leading to innovative solutions that a more closed-off organization might miss. It prompts creativity and collaboration across departments, breaking down the silos that stifle innovation.

Moreover, by making decisions transparent and sharing challenges openly, leaders demonstrate trust in their teams' ability to contribute positively to problem-solving and create space for bold ideas to emerge. Employees are less hesitant to propose new ideas as they see decisions made based on clear, merit-based assessments rather than opaque, hierarchical entitlements.

In conclusion, transparency is not just a managerial buzzword; it is a fundamental requirement for cultivating trust, accountability, and innovation within an organization. By embracing transparency, organizations can create an inclusive culture that encourages shared understanding, collective growth, and sustained success. It is the bedrock upon which integrity and trust are fortified, ensuring that organizational culture remains robust, resilient, and responsive to both opportunities and challenges. However, even the strongest commitment to transparency can be undermined if it coexists with a culture of blame—one of the most damaging forces to trust and innovation.

A pervasive focus on assigning blame rather than learning from failures can cripple an organization's ability to innovate. When employees fear retribution for errors, mistakes become buried under layers of secrecy, robbing the organization of valuable learning opportunities. A blame-oriented mindset is one of the most insidious obstacles to fostering a healthy organizational culture. This approach prioritizes finger-pointing over collaborative problem-solving, slowly eroding trust, creativity, and collective responsibility. When organizations operate under the shadow of blame, they create an environment where fear overshadows innovation, and employees become more concerned with self-preservation than proactive engagement.

In a blame-oriented culture, fear replaces curiosity. Employees avoid taking risks or reporting errors—not out of carelessness, but out of self-preservation. The result? Innovation stalls, communication shuts down, and trust withers.

Leaders in such environments often unwittingly reinforce the blame culture. Instead of modeling accountability and promoting a learning environment, they may resort to punitive measures. Effective leaders should focus on creating a just culture—one that encourages learning from mistakes rather than punishing them. This shift not only helps retain talent but also fosters an atmosphere that promotes transparency and generates trust.

Overcoming a blame-oriented mindset requires deliberate cultural change driven by leaders committed to transparency and openness. Establishing a culture where mistakes are viewed as learning opportunities can ignite a transformative process. Encouraging open dialogue, promoting cross-functional collaboration, and recognizing individual and team contributions help dissipate the fear and defensiveness that blame culture instills.

Uprooting a blame-oriented mindset and replacing it with a culture that values learning, openness, and teamwork is crucial. It transforms the organization from a place of apprehension to one of shared vision and mutual respect, unlocking its full potential to innovate and excel.

Beyond blame, inconsistency breeds its own form of distrust—when policies change without explanation or vary between teams, confusion and resentment take root. Encouraging openness and collaboration is important, but what happens when the systems and policies in place send mixed signals?

Inconsistent policies within an organization can quietly unravel its cultural fabric, leaving confusion, resentment, and disengagement in their wake. These inconsistencies, whether in procedural matters, enforcement, or communication, can significantly damage employee morale and overall trust in the workplace.

When policies are not applied consistently, they create an environment marked by unpredictability. Employees may feel uncertain about expectations, leading to anxiety and reduced confidence in their roles. This uncertainty can breed dissatisfaction as staff members struggle with unclear or shifting objectives.

When employees perceive that policies are not enforced uniformly, it can lead to feelings of favoritism or bias. This perception undermines trust in leadership, creating an environment where employees believe certain individuals are unfairly advantaged. Trust is a foundational component of a healthy workplace culture, and without it, the coherence of the organization is jeopardized.

Inconsistent policy enforcement can also impair accountability. Employees may find it challenging to discern what is expected of them when policies are subject to whimsical changes. This lack of clarity reduces their ability to own their roles fully and hampers their willingness to take initiative, ultimately stifling innovation and responsibility.

A coherent set of policies can drive an organization's values and mission. However, inconsistency not only blurs these goals but may also stymie innovation. Employees might hesitate to pursue new ideas if there is no clear understanding of how they will be evaluated and rewarded, fearing that inconsistent policy application could negate their efforts.

Addressing inconsistency requires concerted effort from leadership to document, communicate, and enforce policies uniformly across all levels of the organization. Training leaders to apply policies consistently and providing forums for feedback can help align understanding and expectations. This proactive approach fosters an equitable environment, restoring trust and encouraging each individual to engage fully and confidently in their roles.

Consistent policies provide the necessary framework for employees to thrive. They assure employees of a fair and predictable environment, encouraging engagement, innovation, and loyalty—key elements for a resilient and dynamic organizational culture. However, even the best policies can falter if day-to-day management undermines them. While a clear framework sets the stage for success, how leaders interact with their teams plays an equally critical role. When leadership veers into micromanagement, it can unravel the very culture those policies aim to support.

The management style of over-controlling supervisors, often characterized by micromanagement, can rapidly deplete employee morale and productivity. In such environments, it strips employees of their autonomy and stifles their ability to demonstrate creativity and initiative.

When supervisors delve into minute details, they inadvertently communicate a lack of trust in their team's capabilities. This not only demoralizes employees but also hampers their job satisfaction and engagement. When employees feel their judgment is undervalued, morale plummets, leading them to disengage, retreat from creativity, and only do what's required—nothing more.

Micromanagement breeds dependency and stifles innovation by fostering an environment where employees hesitate to make independent decisions. This behavior is often rooted in fear of potential scrutiny or reprimand, leading to a stagnant atmosphere devoid of fresh ideas and individual growth. Employees rely on supervisors for direction, diminishing their creative capacities and reducing critical thinking. This cycle undermines a team's potential, as the freedom to explore and propose innovative solutions is suppressed under the weight of overbearing oversight and a lack of constructive feedback.

Over-controlling supervisors restrict communication by creating an environment where employees fear speaking up. This silence leads to unresolved issues, growing misunderstandings, and mounting resentment, breaking down team collaboration and cohesion.

To remediate the effects of micromanagement, organizations must cultivate a culture of trust and empowerment. Supervisors should focus on setting clear expectations and outcomes while allowing their teams the freedom to find the best paths to achieve them. Leadership training should emphasize delegation, active listening, and support for team autonomy. Creating an open feedback loop, where employees feel safe to share ideas and receive constructive feedback, is crucial.

When the organizational culture deteriorates, trust diminishes, engagement wanes, and innovation stagnates. As productivity declines, turnover begins to rise. Safety and creativity, both key drivers of operational excellence, become compromised.

Leaders aiming to revitalize their organizations must actively enable open communication, ensuring every voice is heard and valued. They should cultivate a just culture focused on learning from mistakes rather than punishing them. Empowering leaders at all levels is essential, allowing for decision-making and accountability that drive continuous improvement. Maintaining consistency in policies clarifies expectations, reducing perceived inequalities and nurturing a fair, secure environment.

Through these strategies, organizations can transition from a culture of control to one that prioritizes trust, innovation, and employee development. This shift not only boosts morale but also enhances overall productivity and organizational success, creating a vibrant and resilient workplace.

One notable case study demonstrating the transformation of a company's culture is the story of Microsoft's cultural overhaul under the leadership of CEO Satya Nadella. When Nadella took over as CEO in 2014, Microsoft faced significant challenges concerning its internal culture, which was often described as competitive and lacking collaboration. The company needed change to foster innovation and cooperation across its global teams.

Prior to Nadella's leadership, Microsoft had cultivated a compliance-driven culture. This environment fostered siloed operations where teams were more focused on internal competition than on collaboration and innovation. The legendary stack ranking performance review system, where every unit compared members against each other, entrenched a mindset that deterred teamwork. Employees refrained from sharing information openly, and the culture of fear inhibited risk-taking and creativity—critical elements for a tech company's success.

Nadella's approach to cultural change began with his belief in a 'growth mindset,' a concept developed by Stanford psychologist Carol Dweck. He encouraged employees to view their skills and intelligence as malleable, fostering a culture that was resilient and open to continual learning. One of his first acts as CEO was to replace stack ranking with a performance management system focused on maximizing individual potential and encouraging teamwork.

Empathy became a cornerstone of Microsoft's revitalized culture. Nadella led by example, often emphasizing the importance of understanding one another's perspectives during meetings, product development, and customer interactions. Engineering teams were urged to collaborate both internally and externally, collectively focusing on the mission to empower every individual and organization on the planet to achieve more. This shift necessitated dismantling rigid hierarchical structures and promoting transparency and dialogue at all levels.

Furthermore, Nadella championed diversity and inclusion initiatives, believing that a diverse workforce would drive innovation and improve decision-making. Programs were introduced to enhance gender and racial diversity, while Microsoft's global inclusion policy was strengthened to ensure every employee felt valued and heard. These initiatives, along with measures to encourage employee feedback and adapt policies based on these insights, demonstrated a genuine commitment to evolving the company culture.

The results of these efforts were transformative. Microsoft re-emerged as a leading technology company, rejuvenating its image and product offerings. The focus on cooperation and openness led to advancements such as the integration of cloud services and an increased emphasis on cross-platform development—areas previously considered secondary in a Windows-dominant era.

This cultural evolution faced challenges, requiring consistent reinforcement from leadership and a willingness to address resistance directly. Over time, the commitment to a collaborative and inclusive culture transformed Microsoft into a more agile, innovative, and high-performing organization, contributing to significant financial growth and increased market capitalization during Nadella's tenure.

Microsoft's shift from a compliance-heavy culture to one of trust and empowerment illustrates how addressing culture killers—such as internal competition, lack of communication, and exclusionary practices—can lead to transformative results. This case exemplifies how a clear leadership vision, executed consistently and supported by comprehensive strategies, can foster a more resilient and dynamic workplace.

The journey of Microsoft shows that cultural change isn't just about slogans; it's about making tough, intentional choices. So, what might be quietly undermining your team's success? Identifying and addressing these cultural pitfalls is essential as we transition to explore more examples of effective transformation. Implement changes that will help shape a more resilient organizational culture.

Numerous success stories highlight the power of confronting culture killers head-on. Consider ABC Inc., a company that faced high turnover and declining productivity due to a lack of transparency and pervasive micromanagement. By adopting a more inclusive approach, sharing information freely, and granting employees autonomy, they transformed their toxic culture into one of collaboration and innovation. Employee satisfaction soared, and the company's bottom line reflected this positive shift, with ABC Inc. reducing turnover by 30% and improving employee engagement scores within a year of prioritizing transparency and autonomy.

Recognizing and addressing culture killers is crucial for building and sustaining a culture of trust, ownership, and continuous improvement.

Reflecting on organizations like Microsoft and XYZ Corporation, we see that achieving a positive workplace culture requires more than surface-level solutions. By rooting out and overcoming culture killers, organizations can transform toxic environments into thriving hubs of innovation and growth.

Now that we've uncovered some of the hidden traps that can erode a strong workplace culture, it's time to get practical. In the next chapter, we'll focus on the heartbeat of any manufacturing operation—the frontline leaders. These individuals, whether supervisors, superintendents, foremen, leads, or department managers, play a pivotal role in operational success. As we explore strategies and insights tailored for those navigating day-to-day operations, expect solutions grounded in clarity, trust, and responsibility. We'll connect these concepts to our understanding of culture killers, emphasizing how frontline leadership can counteract these issues through informed, decisive action. Culture killers don't vanish on their own—but with awareness, courage, and consistency, they can be replaced with the very behaviors that drive excellence.

CHAPTER 16:
FRONT-LINE LEADERS

"Companies don't have one culture. They have as many as they have supervisors or managers. You want to build a strong culture? Hold every manager accountable for the culture that he or she builds."
– Marcus Buckingham

Imagine this: Sarah, a dedicated team player who has spent years on the production floor, is suddenly thrust into a new role as a front-line supervisor. Just last week, she was sharing coffee breaks and weekend plans with her colleagues. Today, she stands at the helm, tasked with guiding her team through deadlines and safety checks, balancing camaraderie with authority. This transition is not just a change in title but comes with the weight of new responsibilities that feel both exhilarating and daunting.

Sarah's journey encapsulates the universal challenge faced by many newly minted supervisors: transforming from a peer to a leader while maintaining the balance between influence and responsibility. Initially, she confronts skepticism from her former peers, who now scrutinize her every decision. She quickly realizes that the skills that secured her promotion must now evolve to validate her new position.

As Sarah navigates her early days, she frequently encounters moments of doubt. "Am I cut out for this?" she ponders during a particularly tough meeting. Her initial feelings of powerlessness—common among those newly in charge—are both intimidating and real. Yet, Sarah's story is not unique; it reflects the often-hidden struggles front-line supervisors face when stepping up to their new roles.

While Sarah is no longer on the floor, her understanding of frontline operations becomes her strength. Her previous experience allows her to empathize with her team, serving as a powerful tool in bridging the gap between management's expectations and workers' realities. This ability to influence without direct control becomes her guiding beacon, illustrating the essence of leading from the middle.

Embracing her dual role requires not just grit but a strategic approach to leadership that prioritizes safety, efficiency, and morale—set against the backdrop of ever-present deadlines. In doing so, Sarah learns that leadership is less about asserting control and more about fostering an environment where her team feels empowered to halt operations if safety is compromised.

Sarah's growth into her role underscores a critical takeaway: effective middle-tier leadership hinges on the ability to influence change and reinforce expectations rather than enforce rules. Through her story, we explore how the journey from peer to leader, though fraught with challenges, can be navigated successfully with the right mindset and strategies. As we dig deeper into this chapter, the narrative will illuminate these strategies, equipping current and aspiring supervisors with the skills needed to transition smoothly into their roles.

Sarah's experience provides a compelling entry point into a broader conversation about what it truly takes to step confidently into a leadership role. Building on the insights her journey reveals, we can now take a closer look at concrete strategies that support this transition and help supervisors thrive in their new responsibilities.

Sarah's journey highlights the common challenges many supervisors face during their transitions. Preparing for such a leap requires intentional development. As you step into your new role, clarify your responsibilities and make them visible to your team. Strengthen your leadership with structured experiences, such as workshops focused on leadership techniques and effective communication. Embrace mentoring opportunities, either by pairing with experienced leaders or engaging in job shadowing for deeper insights into leadership dynamics. Simulations of real-world scenarios can further enhance practical decision-making skills.

Consistent feedback mechanisms are crucial for ongoing growth, providing constructive evaluations that encourage learning and improvement. Leverage available leadership resources, whether through reading materials or digital tools, to enhance your effectiveness. As you grow into your role, ensure fairness and consistency in applying expectations, building credibility by making clear what your team can expect. This fostered trust lays the foundation for a successful transition from peer to leader.

Front-line leaders are not just task managers—they shape culture daily. By equipping them with the right tools and perspectives, they become powerful agents of change who bring strategy to life on the floor. This truth becomes especially vivid when we step into the real-world experiences of people like Alex.

In the bustling environment of a large manufacturing plant in Houston, Alex found himself recently promoted from a frontline worker to a supervisor. His transition brought mixed emotions—excitement about the opportunity to lead and anxiety about asserting authority over his former peers. Alex recognized his crucial role, positioned between executing top-level directives and managing the hands-on tasks of the production floor.

One morning, during a routine safety briefing, Alex noticed the anxiety on his team's faces. They were worried about heavy machinery that had recently shown signs of wear. Previously, Alex might have brushed off such concerns, hesitant to challenge higher-ups. But now, equipped with new strategies for upward leadership, he decided to address the issue directly.

Armed with facts, he approached his manager. "I understand the tight deadlines we're under," Alex began, "but I believe pausing operations momentarily to resolve this machinery issue will prevent potential safety hazards and maintain long-term productivity." He backed his case with detailed data on previous downtime costs versus precautionary measures.

Impressed by Alex's initiative and clear presentation, his manager agreed to a temporary halt in operations. Alex didn't stop there. He convened with his team, discussing the planned safety checks openly and encouraging input. "I'm aware we've been pushed to the limit, but ensuring our safety is the first step toward achieving consistent results," he reaffirmed, drawing on his peers' trust and cooperation.

By prioritizing safety and leading with transparency, Alex earned respect across the board. His actions sparked a shift toward a more open, empowered culture—one that made safety the foundation of performance.

As a result, Alex's approach improved not just immediate conditions but also initiated a cultural shift toward a more open, safety-first environment. His ability to navigate the middle ground with influence and effective communication became a template for others facing similar challenges, demonstrating that leadership often involves facilitating proactive dialogue and driving positive change from within. Alex has since been promoted to Operations Director.

One exemplary case study demonstrating the transformative power of investing in frontline supervisors comes from the energy company, Shell. In the early 2000s, Shell faced significant challenges in maintaining safety standards across its global operations. The company realized that adhering to compliance-driven metrics was insufficient for ensuring safety and operational excellence. They required a more profound change in their leadership approach, especially among middle management.

Shell initiated a comprehensive program called "Frontline Leadership Development," targeting supervisors who directly impact day-to-day operational safety. This program aimed not only to enhance supervisory skills but also to nurture these leaders as proactive safety ambassadors within the company.

In the petroleum industry, safety is paramount. Shell's leadership understood that accidents, even minor ones, can have catastrophic consequences. At that time, Shell's safety performance matched industry standards, but they aspired to achieve excellence beyond compliance.

Shell identified a leadership gap in executing safety on the ground and responded with a program blending leadership training, mentorship, and culture change. Frontline leaders received training to develop both technical and leadership skills and were paired with mentors to enhance their capabilities. Consequently, Shell saw improved safety statistics and a reduction in incident rates, demonstrating the effectiveness of investing in leadership development.

Furthermore, Shell's holistic approach yielded a competitive advantage. The company noticed improvements in overall business performance, as a safer working environment led to higher productivity and reduced operational disruptions.

Shell's case underscores the critical role that leadership at the middle management level plays in transforming an organization's culture. By investing in their supervisors, Shell not only boosted safety performance but also set a benchmark for the industry. The initiative demonstrated how developing leaders to engage and inspire their teams can create a sustainable, high-performing organizational culture.

In a broader context, Shell's efforts illustrate that moving beyond compliance in safety to a trust-based leadership model requires intentional investment in people. Organizations aiming to replicate Shell's success should recognize the long-term benefits of nurturing their frontline and middle management with comprehensive expertise that blends technical and leadership skills.

However, this shift toward a trust-based safety culture cannot be sustained or fully realized without the active involvement of frontline leaders. These individuals are the critical link between organizational vision and daily execution—they translate high-level strategies into actionable behaviors and shape how culture is experienced on the ground. Without their buy-in, competence, and consistent reinforcement, even the most well-intentioned cultural initiatives can falter. Frontline supervisors set the tone for team dynamics, model a people-first, safety-always behavior, and serve as the first point of contact when issues arise. If they are not adequately trained or empowered, the culture will remain aspirational rather than operational. Therefore, structured leadership development is not just a value-add—it is a strategic necessity to embed and sustain the kind of culture that Shell and other high-performing organizations strive to achieve.

Without structured leadership training, the potential impacts can be detrimental: Supervisors may lack essential skills to motivate and manage teams, leading to ineffective leadership that fails to inspire or maintain employee morale. Inadequate handling of conflicts or decision-making may prompt employees to leave, influencing team stability and increasing hiring costs. Without an understanding of how to prioritize and integrate safety into daily operations, incidents may rise, risking team well-being and company reputation. By investing in comprehensive training programs and certifications, organizations can significantly enhance their leaders' abilities, ensuring a safer, more productive, and harmonious workplace.

It's easy for frontline leaders to get caught up in the pressure of hitting production targets—but it's worth pausing to consider the deeper impact of your role. The atmosphere on the floor, the way your team communicates, and how safe people feel—physically and psychologically—all stem from your day-to-day leadership. When leadership is driven solely by output, it can unintentionally signal that numbers matter more than people. But when you lead with intention, prioritizing people, safety, and culture, you create an environment where performance naturally follows. That's why frontline supervisors are not just managers—they are culture carriers. Here's why making safety a true cornerstone of your leadership approach is essential:

- A supervisor's most pressing responsibility is to ensure the well-being of their team. By prioritizing safety, leaders protect employees from potential hazards and create an environment conducive to productivity. This proactive approach reduces accidents, leading to fewer disruptions and a more stable operational flow.
- Employees must trust that their supervisors care about their well-being. By consistently placing people and safety first, supervisors

build trust and boost team morale. When workers know that their safety is valued more than deadlines or quotas, they are more likely to be engaged and committed to their roles.

- Compliance with safety regulations is mandatory. However, truly effective leaders view these regulations as a baseline. By striving to exceed these standards, supervisors demonstrate a commitment to excellence and integrity, setting an example that can inspire the entire organization.

- Providing regular safety training and encouraging open discussions about safety practices empowers employees to take ownership of their safety. This empowerment can lead to more vigilant workers who proactively identify and address safety concerns before they escalate into bigger issues.

- Prioritizing safety can lead to significant financial savings by reducing costs associated with workplace injuries, such as medical expenses, fines, and increased insurance premiums. Moreover, a safe work environment can improve productivity and efficiency, directly affecting the bottom line.

- By continuously evaluating and improving safety practices, supervisors can foster a culture of continuous improvement. This mindset encourages innovation and collective responsibility, motivating employees to find better, safer ways to perform their tasks.

As a frontline supervisor, you play a crucial role in establishing a culture where safety is paramount. This isn't just about having the authority to stop work when something feels off—it's about embodying the responsibility to ensure that every procedure is performed under safe conditions. Here, we explore the profound impact of modeling desired behaviors for safety and why every team member should feel empowered with stop work authority. Let's dive into how you can lead by example and encourage a proactive safety culture.

Imagine you, as a supervisor, pause a project because the environment doesn't meet safety standards. Your decisive action sends a powerful message to your team: safety is non-negotiable. By modeling this behavior, you cultivate a workplace where colleagues feel justified and encouraged to voice concerns or halt operations at the slightest hint of danger.

When you visibly prioritize safety, it influences not just your immediate team; it resonates throughout the entire organization. Leaders who regularly demonstrate a commitment to safety inspire others to do the same. This not only reinforces safe practices but also builds an atmosphere of mutual respect and trust. Everyone begins to understand that their decisions, like those of their supervisors, can affect the safety dynamics of their work environment.

Many leaders discuss Stop Work Authority—and rightly so. It's a critical tool for keeping people safe. Stop Work Authority empowers individuals to pause when something feels unsafe.

But what about the decision to begin? Start Work Authority means taking responsibility before a job starts—confirming that conditions are right, risks are understood, and everyone is ready. It's the proactive counterpart to the reactive stance of Stop Work.

When was the last time you—or someone on your team—actually stopped a task because something didn't feel right? When was the last time you or a team member chose not to start because something felt off? Leaders should frequently ask these questions.

That kind of courage is powerful. Let's also encourage our teams to take ownership of the start just as confidently. Leaders, let's discuss both aspects. Let's build a mindset that emphasizes it's not just okay to stop—it's essential to know when and how to start.

Promote a mindset where every team member feels empowered to say, "Let's wait," when conditions aren't normal and, equally important, feels confident to start or resume work when it is safe. This concept—Start Work Authority—highlights that everyone plays a role in initiating work under safe, verified conditions. It validates the voices of all employees and makes them integral to the safety protocol.

Before each shift, remind your team: 'You have the power to speak up. If something doesn't feel right, your judgment matters.' These simple words reinforce collective commitment and the importance of proactive safety.

Incorporate scenario-based training where team members practice decision-making in simulated unsafe conditions. This hands-on approach empowers them to make informed choices, reinforcing the belief that their safety insights are valued. Through simulations, both stopping and starting work becomes a structured process everyone can practice until it becomes second nature.

Open lines of communication are imperative. Make regular check-ins a habit—these are opportunities to discuss upcoming tasks and ensure the team feels supported in prioritizing safety. Reinforce that reporting unsafe conditions is seen as proactive diligence, not disruptive caution.

Supervisors who model stopping operations for safety reasons aren't just acting out of obligation—they're advocating for a holistic approach where safety permeates every decision.

This framework promotes a comprehensive model of safety: it comes full circle when everyone is empowered to halt risky operations and confidently commence work when it's safe to do so.

When supervisors lead with consistent, safety-first actions, they create a center of gravity around which culture forms—anchoring their teams in shared values and expectations.

In many organizations, one of the toughest conversations for a front-line supervisor or employee involves telling a leader that operations aren't running. A good leader should be prepared to accept bad news and lead effectively. When halting operations for safety, clear communication is crucial. Use straightforward language to convey the pause due to safety concerns, such as "Pausing operations due to a safety issue; please hold tasks." Implement visual cues like lights or barricades to support this decision. Additionally, host quick meetings for clarity, foster two-way communication for ongoing safety evaluation, and follow up with written notices detailing issues and projected resolutions.

By clearly articulating reasons and maintaining open communication, supervisors not only secure operational safety but also foster a culture of transparency and trust. These acts not only mitigate immediate risks but also demonstrate a commitment to workplace safety, encouraging all employees to remain vigilant in their own roles.

Building this kind of trust and accountability is especially important when stepping into a leadership role. One of the most pivotal moments in a professional journey is the transition from peer to leader—a shift that brings its own unique challenges and opportunities. You are now on a different stage with a new audience!

Transitioning from peer to leader is a path filled with challenges and learning curves. It requires a shift in dynamics and a clear understanding of your new role without losing the camaraderie that characterized previous interactions. Here's how to navigate this transition effectively:

- Clearly define your new responsibilities to both yourself and your former peers. It's crucial they understand that your decisions are guided by a broader organizational perspective rather than personal motives.
- Establish professional boundaries sensitively. Communicate openly about the changes in your role while emphasizing your commitment to team success.
- Demonstrate the behaviors and work ethic you wish to see in your team. Your actions will speak louder than directives, earning you respect and credibility.
- Apply rules consistently and fairly across the board. Show your former peers that your leadership style is based on justice and integrity.
- Hold regular meetings where concerns and feedback can be openly discussed. This keeps communication lines open and reduces misconceptions or tensions.
- Even as you enforce new boundaries, maintain an open-door policy where team members feel comfortable approaching you with their issues.
- Collaborative Decision-Making: Include team members in decision-making wherever possible. This not only empowers them but showcases your willingness to listen and value their input, fostering a sense of shared leadership.

Balancing authority while retaining respect can be delicate, but several techniques can help:

- Shift focus from "I am in charge" to "I am here to help us succeed." This mindset shows your dedication to serving the team and championing their growth.

- Practice empathy by acknowledging the individual challenges your team faces. Demonstrating understanding can help mitigate any resentment from role shifts.
- Recognize and celebrate team achievements regularly. Providing positive reinforcement boosts morale and solidifies your role as a supportive leader.
- When challenges arise, offer assistance rather than criticism. Help develop solutions collaboratively.
- Always communicate decisions and the rationale behind them transparently. Maintain ethical standards to reinforce trust and integrity in your leadership.
- Be flexible in your approach, adapting strategies to fit evolving group dynamics and individual personalities.

Navigating from peer to leader is a delicate dance that requires mastering the art of balance—balancing authority with genuine empathy, ensuring that professionalism never comes at the expense of mutual respect and collaboration. By adopting these strategies, new leaders can cultivate an environment that fosters respect, cooperation, and collective success. However, the role of a front-line supervisor doesn't end with managing those beneath them. Equally challenging is the need to influence those above you in the hierarchy. This unique position of being "stuck in the middle" allows you to implement organizational goals at the front line while subtly steering the trajectory of management decisions by aligning your department's goals with broader company objectives. Here, we explore strategies that excel in this upward leadership endeavor, allowing you to communicate effectively with higher management and actively influence organizational direction.

Effectively navigating the dynamics of influencing those higher in the organizational hierarchy involves aligning goals with those of the organization. As a front-line supervisor, illustrating how your team's work supports larger company objectives solidifies your position as a leader in tune with management priorities. Ensure your communications are concise and adapt them to the preferred style of senior management; some respond better to data-backed proposals, while others prefer high-level overviews. Engage with superiors through informal dialogues, establishing rapport beyond professional confines, which can ease future interactions.

Demonstrating reliability by consistently delivering results enhances trust and encourages management to value your ideas. Regularly offer insights from field operations, providing unique perspectives that may aid strategic decisions at higher levels. Finally, support your proposals with compelling data to fortify your position and demonstrate thoroughness.

Reflection and open dialogue not only foster personal growth but also enhance your influence, gradually shaping an efficient, harmonious work environment that benefits the entire organization.

Recently, I spoke with a leader who has traveled the path many of us are on—starting from the ground up and climbing the ladder by implementing these exact strategies. His journey serves as a powerful reminder of what's possible when you remain committed and intentional. Here's how his story unfolded.

This theme of impactful leadership from within the organizational ranks is echoed in Sarah's experience, which provides another compelling perspective on the transformative potential of mid-level leaders.

Sarah's journey brings the chapter full circle. Her progression from peer to leader illustrates how front-line supervisors shape culture through action—by listening, leading with empathy, and prioritizing people.

In fostering a culture of ownership, Sarah's decision to halt operations upon noticing potential dangers exemplifies a proactive approach to leadership. This pivotal choice not only ensures the physical safety of her team but also conveys her commitment to their wellbeing, thereby building trust and confidence among her peers. Her leadership instills an ethos where safety is everyone's priority, making her a role model for those who may feel "stuck in the middle" between workforce expectations and top-tier directives.

Strategic leadership, particularly from the middle, proves powerful in reshaping workplace norms and enhancing overall safety cultures. As Sarah navigated these challenges, she demonstrated that when mid-level supervisors align their actions with safety goals, they can lead profound cultural transformations. This alignment equips them with the influence to improve communication across all levels of the organization while ensuring every team member feels protected and heard. The narrative underscores the critical role of leaders who understand the landscape of front-line operations and can steer it toward safer and more productive outcomes through empathetic and authoritative guidance.

Building on these individual leadership journeys, the next chapter explores how safety can be seamlessly integrated into the fabric of everyday operations. Rather than treating safety as a standalone initiative, this section delves into practical strategies, cultural reinforcements, and structural changes that embed safety into routine decision-making, behaviors, and team dynamics across all levels of the organization.

Before diving into the next chapter, take a moment to reflect on your own day-to-day operations.

Is safety part of your team's DNA—or a poster on the wall? Do you lead in a manner that makes safety visible in every action, every decision, every moment? How can you take one step this week to make safety more instinctive—for yourself and your team?

These aren't just questions—they're opportunities to pause, refocus, and consider how to make safety not just a policy, but a mindset. Let's explore how to embed it into the heartbeat of your operations.

CHAPTER 17:
EMBEDDING SAFETY

"The problem isn't so much finding good ideas (there is no shortage) as embedding the ones we have into everyday practice."
– Alain de Botton

Have you ever wondered whether safety is genuinely part of your daily operations—or just a box to check? This chapter explores what it means to truly embed safety into the fabric of an organization, starting with a powerful example: how Alaska Airlines transformed safety into the heartbeat of their business.

In high-risk industries, the aviation sector exemplifies rigorous safety practices. However, Alaska Airlines emerged as a transformative figure by integrating safety into its core operations in an unparalleled manner. This case study reveals how Alaska Airlines, once criticized for safety lapses, evolved into a leader in safety by embedding it into every facet of its operations—not as a standalone department, but as the company's heartbeat.

The narrative begins in the late 1990s, a turbulent period for Alaska Airlines. In January 2000, the airline experienced a tragic incident when Flight 261 crashed into the Pacific Ocean, resulting in the loss of 88 lives. Investigations revealed lapses in maintenance and a culture that prioritized operations over safety. This catastrophic event served as a wake-up call, prompting a complete overhaul of the company's safety strategy.

Brad Tilden, who joined the company in 1991 and later became CEO in 2012, was instrumental in steering this transformation. Following the incident, Alaska Airlines committed to not merely complying with Federal Aviation Administration (FAA) regulations but exceeding them. This mindset marked the transition from a compliance-driven approach to a trust-centered safety culture.

In 2016, the FAA formally accepted the Safety Management Systems (SMS) of Alaska Airlines and Horizon Air, marking a milestone in how modern carriers can lead in safety—not just comply with regulations. While all U.S. airlines were required under a 2015 FAA rule to implement SMS programs by January 2018, Alaska and Horizon were already years ahead. Both airlines had fully implemented their systems by 2012, while the FAA was still validating the framework.

The adoption of SMS at Alaska and Horizon illustrates the meaning of going beyond compliance. Rather than treating safety as a regulatory checkbox or the responsibility of a single department, the airlines built a safety culture that permeates every level of the organization. This comprehensive approach empowers all 15,600 employees across both carriers to actively participate in risk identification, assessment, and mitigation. Every employee is trained in safety protocols and—most notably—authorized to stop operations if a concern arises.

This early adoption laid the foundation for a company-wide mindset shift—driven by leadership—that redefined safety not as a constraint, but as a core value.

"Engineering safety into our culture and every part of our business" was how Alaska Airlines President and COO Ben Minicucci described it. His counterpart at Horizon, President and CEO David Campbell, emphasized the empowerment of frontline staff as the "bedrock of safety improvements."

This shift from a compliance-based mindset to a culture-driven model produced tangible results. In the same year the FAA formally accepted their SMS programs, Alaska became the first commercial airline in the world to receive FAA certification for a full-stall flight simulator—an advanced training tool to help pilots practice critical recovery skills. Both airlines also received their 15th Diamond Award of Excellence from the FAA, recognizing their outstanding commitment to maintenance training. Meanwhile, a team of Alaska's maintenance technicians took first place in the national Aerospace Maintenance Competition, highlighting the operational depth of their safety capabilities.

Tom Nunn, Vice President of Safety, emphasized the crucial role of SMS for future improvements, stating that these systems provide a foundation for ongoing progress rather than solely functioning as compliance tools. "SMS will be a big part of our future," he stated. By offering a platform to swiftly adapt and continuously learn, SMS allows teams to analyze risk patterns and anticipate and address emerging challenges. Such systems nurture an environment where safety protocols are dynamically refined and integrated into daily operations, driving both cultural and procedural enhancements throughout the organization.

Building upon Tom Nunn's emphasis on SMS for sustained safety improvements, the integration of the Safety Information Management System (SIMS) and Operational Safety Risk Management (OSRM) offers tangible pathways to advance these goals. SIMS serves as a comprehensive digital platform that democratizes safety data, empowering all stakeholders, from pilots to mechanics, to actively participate in identifying and addressing safety issues. By fostering a transparent reporting culture, SIMS encourages open dialogue and accountability.

Meanwhile, OSRM takes a proactive stance, systematically identifying potential risks and facilitating preventive measures across all organizational levels. Together, SIMS and OSRM transform safety from a static compliance requirement into a dynamic, integral part of organizational operations, promoting both cultural and procedural growth.

It fostered transparency and accountability through a robust reporting culture. Employees were encouraged—and incentivized—to report safety issues without fear of retribution, thereby building trust and collaboration.

To cultivate a mindset of safety, the company launched the "Flight Plan" initiative. This involved quarterly meetings where executives and frontline workers discussed safety metrics in an open forum. The dialogue was candid and constructed a narrative linking safety with success metrics directly, such as punctuality and customer satisfaction.

Leadership played a pivotal role in transforming the safety culture. They adopted a "walk-around" approach, enabling executives to interact directly with employees at all levels and understand the safety challenges on the ground. This practice underscored management's commitment and authenticity, bridging the gap between policy and practice.

Partnerships with labor unions underscored the collaborative approach adopted by Alaska Airlines. By aligning with pilot and maintenance unions, whose interests often clash with management, they established protocols that prioritized human factors and risk management. This collaboration streamlined safety procedures and improved alignment between leadership and labor.

Training became a central tenet of Alaska Airlines' safety evolution. The airline embraced advanced simulation-based training for pilots and crew, focusing on situational awareness and decision-making in critical scenarios. This hands-on training equipped employees with the confidence and skills to react quickly and calmly in real-life emergencies. Furthermore, Alaska Airlines collaborated with industry experts to develop training that extended beyond technical skills to include leadership and communication, reinforcing the idea that safety is a shared endeavor.

Over the years, Alaska Airlines' transformation yielded tangible results. By 2008, they had drastically reduced flight cancellations and minimized significant incidents, earning numerous accolades for their safety initiatives. It was not just about metrics—it was about fostering an organizational culture where every employee felt like a guardian of safety.

These internal changes benefited not only employees and operations but also reshaped Alaska Airlines' image within the industry. This metamorphosis extended beyond internal operations to external brand perception. The airline gained a reputation for innovative safety practices in the aviation community, often sharing insights and contributing to industry-wide safety enhancements. Their model became a benchmark for other airlines, demonstrating that true safety leadership transcends compliance, cultivating a culture where safety is woven into the very fabric of daily operations.

Recognized by the FAA for their proactive safety measures, Alaska Airlines set a precedent that safety must be a core value, integral to every decision-making level. Their journey illustrates that in high-risk industries, leadership must champion safety to inspire trust and enhance organizational resilience.

This example shows that safety leadership is not defined by regulatory deadlines, but by how deeply an organization embeds safety into its identity. Alaska and Horizon's journey is a powerful case study in leading for safety—not because it's required, but because it's right.

Incorporating safety as a core component of daily operations is critical to becoming the best organization possible. Transitioning from an isolated safety protocol to an embedded cultural element is not only beneficial—it is pivotal for sustainable success, especially in high-stakes industries like aviation. Here, we explore practical strategies to achieve this shift.

Creating a culture that prioritizes safety begins with an organization-wide mindset that regards safety as a shared principle and value. This requires leadership commitment at the highest levels to foster a people-first, safety-always mindset. Companies can implement regular safety training sessions and workshops that are compulsory for all employees, regardless of their role. Additionally, establishing open communication channels for reporting and discussing safety concerns without fear of reprisal encourages a proactive approach to safety.

Operationalizing safety necessitates collaboration across all departments. It involves designing integrated systems where safety protocols are ingrained in every operational workflow. Employing cross-functional teams to regularly audit safety measures ensures that safety considerations are factored into every aspect of operation—from planning to execution.

To keep safety measures aligned with the latest industry standards, continuous learning should be integral to operational philosophy. This involves staying informed about new technologies and practices through participation in industry safety forums and adapting lessons learned from incidents to enhance existing protocols. By establishing feedback loops across the organization, companies can continuously refine their safety strategies based on real-world outcomes and evolving knowledge.

The integration of safety into everyday operations is critical for the success and sustainability of any organization, especially in high-risk industries such as aviation. At the heart of embedding safety into the fabric of daily activities is leadership. Leaders set the tone, create the culture, and allocate the resources necessary to ensure that safety becomes an intrinsic part of organizational operations rather than an afterthought.

Leadership commitment is the cornerstone of embedding safety into operations. Leaders should model safety behaviors—whether through walk-arounds, audits, or team check-ins—to show that safety is not optional but integral to success. By creating feedback loops, engaging with employees, and making safety visible in every action, they build a culture where safety becomes an intrinsic value, not just a checklist.

To embed safety deeply, leaders must cultivate a culture where safety is seen as a shared responsibility. This involves promoting open communication and feedback loops where employees feel empowered to voice safety concerns without fear of retaliation. Leaders can facilitate workshops, safety training sessions, and team-building exercises that reinforce safety as a collaborative effort, emphasizing that each employee plays a critical role in maintaining a secure environment.

Effective leaders ensure that adequate resources are dedicated to safety initiatives. This includes investing in advanced safety technologies, ongoing training programs, and systems to monitor and report safety performance. By prioritizing budget allocations for safety, leaders underscore its importance and demonstrate a commitment to not just meeting regulatory requirements but exceeding them.

Great leaders emphasize the importance of safety in every decision, aligning operational procedures with the organization's safety mindset. Additionally, they actively engage with employees at all levels, soliciting their input on safety improvements and incorporating frontline insights into safety strategies. This involvement not only enhances the efficacy of safety protocols but also fosters a sense of ownership and accountability among the workforce.

When safety becomes a seamless part of how work gets done, organizations don't just reduce risk—they unlock greater efficiency, stronger engagement, and long-term resilience. By embedding safety as a fundamental part of work processes, organizations can enhance operational efficiency, reduce downtime, and foster a proactive work culture. Below are detailed insights into how safety integration leads to increased productivity.

Integrating safety into everyday operations leads to significant reductions in downtime caused by accidents or unsafe conditions. When safety is prioritized, equipment is maintained, and potential hazards are proactively addressed, resulting in fewer interruptions to workflow. With fewer incidents, companies can maintain continuous operations, naturally improving productivity.

Employees who feel safe in their workplace are more engaged and efficient. When organizations invest in comprehensive safety programs, they demonstrate a commitment to employee well-being, fostering a positive work environment where employees are more attentive, confident, and productive. High morale and reduced stress levels lead to improved focus and efficiency in tasks.

Implementing safety measures minimizes workplace injuries, which can be costly in terms of medical expenses and legal liabilities. By reducing the frequency and severity of accidents, organizations save financial resources that can be redirected towards improving processes and investing in technology that further boosts productivity.

Consider a mid-sized automotive parts manufacturer that implemented monthly cross-functional safety audits coupled with incentive programs. Within two years, workplace incidents dropped by 30%, and employee satisfaction surveys reflected a 40% increase in perceived safety support.

Embedding safety into the core of daily operations enhances productivity, minimizes risk, and strengthens trust across the organization. In fast-paced environments, it's easy to lose sight of safety amid deadlines—but when safety becomes a shared mindset woven into every action, organizations thrive with greater efficiency, accountability, and resilience.

Drawing on the opening narrative of Alaska Airlines, we can revisit how their meticulous implementation of safety practices serves as a testament to what can be achieved when safety becomes an integral part of everyday operations.

In the bustling corridors of Alaska Airlines, safety isn't an isolated departmental concern—it's a core mindset that permeates every function of the company. The airline's approach serves as a model for operational excellence, where safety protocols enhance productivity rather than hinder it. Alaska Airlines achieved this through a series of strategic initiatives aimed at embedding safety into the daily routines of each team member.

Alaska Airlines introduced an extensive educational program for all employees. This program extended beyond traditional training sessions to include interactive workshops and continuous learning opportunities. This initiative ensured that all staff were up-to-date with the latest safety standards and best practices, creating a workforce confident in their knowledge and capabilities.

The airline made significant investments in technology to enhance safety, utilizing state-of-the-art aircraft monitoring systems and innovative predictive analytics. These technologies not only prevented incidents by identifying potential issues before they emerged but also streamlined maintenance schedules, minimizing delays and disruptions.

What truly distinguishes Alaska Airlines is its culture of safety ownership. Leadership at all levels champions this cause, fostering open communication where employees can report safety concerns without fear. This empowerment creates an environment where vigilance becomes second nature.

As a result of these comprehensive safety practices, Alaska Airlines not only reduced incident rates but also achieved notable improvements in overall operational efficiency. Flights became more reliably on-time, customer satisfaction ratings increased, and employees enjoyed a safer, more supportive work environment.

Alaska Airlines' journey demonstrates that when safety is genuinely embedded in daily practices—from frontline actions to executive decision-making—operational excellence follows. Their story serves as a model for others seeking lasting cultural change.

Alaska Airlines illustrates what's possible when safety transcends policy and becomes a promise. As you reflect on your own operations, consider: how integrated is safety in your daily decisions? Now, let's explore practical steps to cultivate a lasting 'People First, Safety Always' culture in your organization.

CHAPTER 18:
PEOPLE FIRST SAFETY ALWAYS

Sustainability in safety refers to the enduring implementation and maintenance of practices and cultures that protect people, assets, and the environment over time. It involves the continuous adaptation of safety measures to meet changing conditions, technologies, and societal expectations.

In the quest for a steadfast "Safety Always" culture, few companies provide a more compelling case study than DuPont, a science and materials company renowned for its safety performance. For over 200 years, DuPont has evolved its safety protocols, establishing a legacy that speaks volumes about sustaining safety excellence through unwavering commitment and adaptability.

The company's journey began in 1802 with a focus on gunpowder manufacturing, a notoriously dangerous industry. From the outset, founder E.I. du Pont emphasized safety as the paramount principle. His approach was simple yet revolutionary for the time: no profits were worth a life. This philosophy laid the foundation for DuPont's safety, a principle that would grow and adapt over the centuries.

Over the decades, DuPont's commitment to safety evolved alongside its business expansions and technological advancements. The company adopted a proactive approach, continuously enhancing its safety practices to anticipate risks rather than reacting to them. This adaptability became a hallmark of DuPont's strategy, bolstering its reputation as a leader in industrial safety.

A critical aspect of DuPont's sustained excellence has been the implementation of the "DuPont STOP" program, initiated in 1986. STOP—Safety Training Observation Program—was designed to engage both employees and management in recognizing and mitigating unsafe behaviors. The program's focus on observation and constructive feedback cultivated a culture of continuous improvement, empowering employees at all levels to participate in safety discussions.

DuPont's safety principles also extended beyond its own operations. Through its DuPont Sustainable Solutions division, the company provided consultancy, sharing its methodologies and helping other organizations establish their own safety cultures. This not only solidified DuPont's leadership in safety but also demonstrated its adaptability in applying safety principles across various industries.

The impact of DuPont's safety mindset is reflected in its impressive safety record. By the 2000s, the company reported injury rates significantly lower than industry averages. Furthermore, DuPont sustained this success by embedding safety into every facet of its operations. Leadership at all levels prioritized safety, recognizing that a genuine "people-first" approach translates into enhanced productivity and morale.

An illustrative example of adaptability emerged in response to evolving chemical industry regulations and societal expectations. DuPont proactively implemented environmental safety measures that exceeded regulatory requirements, reinforcing its commitment to safety not only for its employees but also for the communities around its facilities. This forward-thinking mindset allowed DuPont to maintain its status as a safety pioneer in an ever-changing industrial landscape.

DuPont's legacy of adaptability and people-first principles lays the groundwork for understanding how other global leaders—like Toyota—achieve similar sustainability through their own cultural pathways.

Building on this foundation of excellence, we can now turn our attention to Toyota, another iconic example of sustained safety culture. Toyota exemplifies how a robust safety culture can evolve through long-term commitment, operational integration, and employee empowerment. Renowned for its dedication to quality, Toyota has seamlessly integrated safety into its core operations, ensuring exemplary standards over decades.

The roots of Toyota's safety culture stem from the Toyota Production System (TPS), established in the early 20th century. TPS emphasizes efficiency, quality, and respect for people, forming the basis for a robust safety environment. Central to this approach is jidoka, or automation with a human touch, which empowers workers to stop the line if something goes wrong. This ensures problems are addressed immediately, preventing unsafe conditions. Alongside this is kaizen, a philosophy of continuous improvement that invites every employee, from line workers to managers, to contribute ideas that enhance workplace safety and efficiency.

This bottom-up approach empowers employees, instilling a sense of ownership over safety processes. Kaizen workshops are routinely held across Toyota plants, promoting discussions around safety measures and collective problem-solving.

The adaptability of Toyota's culture is evident through its response to global challenges. Following the 2011 Fukushima disaster in Japan, Toyota implemented rigorous checks and new protocols to enhance disaster preparedness at its facilities worldwide. This included revisiting supply chain safety and ensuring operational resilience, demonstrating Toyota's commitment to adapting to new safety challenges.

A pivotal aspect of Toyota's sustained safety excellence is its training programs. The company invests significantly in educating employees about safety protocols, safety leadership, and emergency response. This holistic approach ensures all staff, from line workers to executives, are aligned with the company's safety vision.

Toyota's adaptability is further demonstrated in its embrace of technology to enhance safety. With the advent of new automotive technologies, Toyota has incorporated advanced safety features like collision prevention systems and automated driving technologies. These innovations not only ensure vehicle safety but also reflect Toyota's commitment to staying ahead of industry trends to protect the lives of customers and employees.

The impact of Toyota's culture is considerable. Reports indicate that Toyota has achieved industry-low accident rates, a testament to its effective safety practices. This success stems from integrating safety into the cultural fabric of the organization. Toyota views safety not as a separate function but as an integral component of quality and productivity, solidifying its reputation as an industry leader in safety.

To broaden our understanding of sustainability, it's helpful to look beyond traditional workplaces and explore how these principles thrive in unexpected settings like elite sports organizations. Just as Toyota seamlessly integrates safety into its organizational culture, remarkable results in accident rates can be observed in sports. For instance, FC Barcelona's La Masia academy exemplifies a sustainable approach by focusing on developing young talent holistically. This way, sustainability isn't confined to industrial environments but also thrives in diverse areas like sports, nurturing long-term growth and community values.

Unlike many clubs investing heavily in external star players, FC Barcelona has a tradition of nurturing young talent through La Masia—an academy known for transforming players into not only athletes but also well-rounded individuals. This approach emphasizes community, training continuity, and judiciously shared resources over time, fostering sustainability by valuing long-term growth over fleeting success.

La Masia's focus on developing athletes into well-rounded individuals—rather than relying on external talent—parallels how operational excellence is best sustained from within. This inward development fosters a lasting culture of trust and growth, much like organizations that embed safety as a lived value.

Let's examine what it truly takes to maintain a strong culture—one that consistently leads to safe outcomes. You might notice something interesting along the way: many of these elements aren't all that different from what it takes to build the culture in the first place. It often comes down to one core ingredient—People.

Key Elements to Maintaining a Strong Safety Culture

1. Leadership Commitment

- **Model Safety as a Core Value**: Demonstrate safety as non-negotiable through everyday decisions and behaviors.
- **Integrate Safety in Business Strategies**: Align safety goals with business objectives for a cohesive approach.

2. Trust & Transparency

- **Foster Open Dialogue**: Encourage a blame-free environment for discussions around safety concerns.
- **Act and Communicate with Consistency**: Build credibility by maintaining clear and consistent messaging.

3. Employee Involvement

- **Engage Diverse Voices**: Rotate safety committee membership to ensure varied perspectives.
- **Encourage Safety Innovation**: Host contests or idea campaigns focused on enhancing safety practices.

4. Training & Communication

- **Offer Regular Safety Education**: Tailor safety training to meet specific team needs.
- **Reinforce Learning On-the-Floor**: Engage in ongoing safety conversations to solidify understanding.

5. Continuous Improvement

- **Learn from Near Misses and Trends**: Analyze incidents as learning opportunities to enhance practices.
- **Update Policies Regularly**: Share findings and policy updates to foster organizational learning.

6. Accountability

- **Clarify Safety Roles at All Levels**: Define responsibilities comprehensively to promote accountability.
- **Focus on Systems, Not Individuals**: Apply safety policies consistently to ensure systemic accountability.

7. Positive Reinforcement

- **Celebrate Safety Wins Publicly**: Recognize achievements to motivate ongoing safety practices.
- **Share Success Stories**: Illustrate exemplary safety behavior to set benchmarks for others.

Have you ever wondered which pieces of the puzzle matter most in making sustainability stick within a company? Two elements stand out—and they set the tone for everything else: leadership commitment and trust. These aren't nice-to-haves; they form the foundation. Without them, even the best sustainability plans can struggle to take root. However, when they're strong, they shape the culture, drive long-term success, and build resilience from within.

Evaluating DuPont's story reveals clear lessons: a perpetual commitment to safety, coupled with an adaptive approach, ensures sustainability in safety culture. By treating safety as a core value and integrating it into everyday operations, companies can achieve and sustain a "People First - Safety Always" culture. This holistic approach captures the essence of prioritizing people, driving transformative results in both safety and business performance.

As we transition from DuPont to another industrial safety leader, Toyota emerges as a complementary narrative, showcasing how a steadfast commitment to quality can seamlessly incorporate robust safety protocols. Both companies exemplify how adaptability and dedication to safety can drive long-term success. At Toyota, the integration of safety within core operations has been seamless, demonstrating exemplary safety standards that have stood the test of time. This examination underscores the universality of effective cultures while highlighting the diverse paths companies can take to achieve similar outcomes.

In cultivating a transformative safety culture, the common thread across successful organizations is their unwavering commitment to prioritizing people over processes. Safety becomes transformative when seamlessly integrated into the organization's fabric, akin to the DNA that ensures vitality and resilience. This integrated approach not only leads to fewer incidents but also fosters a sense of community where every member feels valued and empowered to contribute to collective well-being.

By adopting a mindset that views safety as a proactive and dynamic process, companies can drive continuous improvement and innovation, creating a sustainable environment that benefits both individuals and the organization. This transformation is not an endpoint but a continual evolution requiring leadership, engagement, and adaptability at all levels.

Ultimately, what sustains a truly transformative safety culture isn't policy—it's people. When organizations champion adaptability, listen deeply, and lead with integrity, safety becomes more than a priority—it becomes a way of life. Let's commit to building cultures where safety is lived daily, driven by trust and sustained by purpose.

Let's challenge ourselves and consider what's truly supporting or obstructing our journey toward safety excellence. Ultimately, it's not the policies that sustain a transformative safety culture—it's the people. When organizations foster adaptability, deeply engage in listening, and lead with integrity, safety evolves into a way of life rather than just a priority. Let's wholeheartedly commit to establishing cultures where safety is not just practiced but lived every day, anchored in trust and driven by purpose. As we move forward into the next chapter, which explores the journey to safety excellence, remember that the true essence of safety leadership is not found in what is mandated, but in what is lived and shared.

CHAPTER 19:
THE JOURNEY

"If you are going to achieve excellence in big things, you develop the habit in little matters. Excellence is not an exception, it is a prevailing attitude."
- Colin Powell

Step into the world of a high-performing manufacturing plant in Iowa— once just another name in their industry, now a model of safety excellence. Through the eyes of Jennifer, a passionate line worker turned catalyst for cultural change, we witness a shift from compliance to conviction. Her story reminds us: true safety isn't about ticking boxes—it's about people, purpose, and trust.

Jennifer began her journey like any other employee, eager yet uncertain of her role's larger impact. When she attended her first safety meeting, she was struck not by what was discussed, but by what was unsaid: the palpable silence around the potential for real change. Motivated not by mandate, but by a burning commitment to her colleagues' well-being, Jennifer's quiet actions initiated a ripple effect. Accountability transformed from an awkward obligation into a deeply integrated belief. Her efforts in rallying her peers, gathering feedback, and spearheading initiatives led to seismic shifts—top down and bottom up.

In the workstations and hallways, safety became synonymous with excellence. Other departments took notice one by one. The light Jennifer ignited spread, and the facility morphed into a model for others grappling with similar transformation needs.

As we embark on this chapter, let's remember that this journey toward true safety excellence is ongoing, dynamic, and built on commitment, passion, people, and leadership rooted in trust.

Safety excellence is more than compliance—it's a dynamic, people-first culture where trust and collaboration drive every decision. Picture a morning briefing where every voice matters, where employees aren't just following protocols but actively shaping them. In such environments, safety isn't an obligation—it's a shared mindset.

This energy stems from a deeply embedded culture where every voice matters. Here, people feel empowered to speak up, share insights, and most importantly, take proactive steps towards ensuring safety. Safety excellence isn't an exercise filled with checklists—it becomes an integral part of the organizational fabric, woven into daily operations and decision-making processes. Grassroots participation often fuels larger systemic change. Some of the natural leaders in your organization are on the production floor!

Consider your production floor—who do people turn to when challenges arise? It's often not the person with the title, but the one who listens, remains calm, and quietly unites others. These unsung leaders earn trust through consistency, not control. Who fits that role on your team?

The cornerstone of safety excellence lies squarely with its people. Each employee, from the CEO to the newest recruit, must feel they are agents of change within their workplace ecosystem. This goes beyond conventional training and periodic meetings; it demands a holistic, inclusive approach that respects and leverages the diverse skills and perspectives team members bring. By fostering an environment where employees are encouraged to identify potential hazards and actively involved in crafting solutions, organizations create a sense of ownership that drives safety performance.

For example, consider a scenario where a frontline worker suggests a process change based on firsthand observations. By integrating such insights, leadership not only safeguards the workforce but also builds trust and accountability.

Cultural transformation towards safety excellence requires nurturing a mindset that safety isn't someone else's job but an organizational responsibility. Leaders play a pivotal role here—not as distant figureheads but as engaged participants who demonstrate commitment through actions, such as open dialogues and recognizing contributions toward safety improvements. When leadership participates actively in safety discussions and visibly champions safety measures, they lead by example, setting a precedent that resonates throughout the organization. Such leadership actions solidify a culture where every individual feels motivated to contribute to the collective safety mission.

To sustain this momentum, organizations must commit to continuous learning and adaptation. Regular feedback loops, flexible safety strategies, and responsive leadership are vital. Moreover, nurturing peer acknowledgment and collaboration ensures the culture remains vibrant and forward-thinking. Safety excellence becomes a moving target, with evolving goals as the organizational environment and technology landscape change.

Ultimately, achieving safety excellence is a dynamic journey driven by an unwavering belief in the power of people and culture. The shared vision of a safe working environment grows only through dedication and collaboration, ensuring it remains resilient against the test of time. As we reflect on the transformative journeys illustrated throughout our narratives, it becomes clear that genuine safety excellence is an ongoing endeavor requiring the collective investment of everyone involved.

As we dig deeper into the evolution of workplace safety, it's crucial to understand the shift from traditional methods to contemporary approaches that emphasize trust and engagement. This journey, intricately woven with individual and collective efforts, mirrors the broader transition from Frederick Taylor's scientific management to today's more human-centric models of safety leadership. Frederick Taylor's early 20th-century model treated workers as components in a machine, optimized for output. While revolutionary for its time, it left little room for trust or individual agency. Today, we recognize that true excellence demands a human-centric approach—one that values insight, participation, and collective responsibility.

The modern work environment endorses a paradigm shift towards trust and engagement, vividly illustrated by the story of NUMMI, a joint venture between General Motors and Toyota. NUMMI exemplifies the transformative power of trust, collaboration, and employee engagement, with a strong emphasis on safety leadership and culture.

Before NUMMI's inception in 1984, the Fremont, California GM plant was notorious for its problematic workforce and substandard quality. The facility closed in 1982 due to high absenteeism, poor morale, and low productivity, emblematic of a Tayloristic management approach that failed to foster trust or engage workers.

Toyota entered the scene with its renowned Toyota Production System, emphasizing quality, respect, continuous improvement, and employee involvement. When the Fremont plant reopened as the New United Motor Manufacturing Inc. (NUMMI), Toyota integrated its philosophy, transforming a combative workforce into one of the most productive in the United States. The success at NUMMI was not merely operational but cultural—achieved through trust and engagement.

The transformation began with Toyota sending a selection of former GM workers to Japan for training. This decision aimed to foster trust and immerse them in Toyota's culture, which valued each worker as a crucial individual capable of contributing to safety and efficiency. Their empowerment contrasted sharply with Taylor's idea of management driven by constant oversight.

Upon returning, the workers brought back not only skills but also an understanding of a collaborative environment. Their voices mattered, and they were encouraged to stop the production line if any safety concerns or quality issues arose. This empowerment fostered a sense of ownership over their work, aligning personal accomplishments with the organization's goals.

The success at NUMMI highlighted key differences between Taylor's rigidity and modern trust-based management. While Taylor's model did not accommodate the nuances of human behavior, NUMMI's approach embraced it, recognizing trust and collaboration as catalysts for superior performance. With enhanced safety practices, productivity increased as workers felt respected and vital to the company's mission.

NUMMI's story illustrates that transforming safety isn't just about new systems—it's about shifting hearts and minds. Their journey underscores an essential truth: cultural change begins with trust, not tools. NUMMI's transition resonated throughout various industries, demonstrating that transforming an organization requires more than new processes; it necessitates building a cultural foundation on trust and partnership. Today, successful organizations recognize the flaws in Taylor's approach of viewing workers as sheer components of machinery. Instead, they strive to cultivate environments where trust fosters passion, creativity, and responsibility.

This shift from compliance-focused safety management to a trust-based approach invites all stakeholders to actively engage in creating safer and more productive workplaces. By transforming employees from spectators into active contributors, organizations enable true ownership of safety and efficiency.

As we move forward, remember that safety excellence isn't a destination—it's an ongoing commitment to people, purpose, and progress. When we build environments rooted in trust and shared ownership, safety becomes more than a protocol—it becomes part of our identity.

The stories recounted in prior chapters carry significant weight: tales of individuals and organizations revamping their approaches and redefining what it means to care. By illustrating these transformative efforts, we envision not just safer workplaces today, but a climate of proactive vigilance for future leaders to inherit.

As you look onward, recognize that your active engagement within these pages isn't just academic—it's a precursor to action. Understand deeply that safety excellence combines all efforts, ever-evolving, and is a collective aim toward which every one of us can and should strive. Ultimately, it's not just compliance—it's culture, it's people, it's passion, and it all begins with trust!

In this evolved framework, safety leaders are envisioned as facilitators of open communication, fostering environments where employees at all levels feel encouraged to voice concerns and propose solutions. This participative approach ensures that safety protocols are not just top-down mandates but collaborative efforts drawing on the collective expertise and experience of the workforce. Furthermore, the future envisions leaders who champion diversity and inclusivity, recognizing that varied perspectives are crucial for identifying comprehensive safety strategies that cater to a diverse workforce.

At the heart of this vision lies a commitment to continuous learning and development—where safety leaders prioritize ongoing education, staying abreast of industry innovations and evolving risks. By championing a community of ubiquitous safety mindfulness, these leaders inspire a workforce that views safety as a shared responsibility integral to both organizational success and personal well-being.

The future of safety leadership resides at the intersection of empathy and innovation. As technologies like AI and predictive analytics evolve, so too must our leadership—grounded in emotional intelligence, inclusivity, and collaboration. The leaders of tomorrow won't just manage risks; they'll nurture cultures where every person feels seen, heard, and empowered to lead in safety.

As we stand on the cliff of understanding safety excellence, we realize it's not just about reaching a destination but navigating a continuous journey grounded in trust, people, and a shared vision. Imagine a culture where everyone takes ownership, where adaptability isn't just a buzzword but a way of life, and where safety isn't viewed as a protocol but a pulse—constant, steady, reliable. In stepping forward, let's turn our attention to the metrics we rely on. Do they accurately reflect our values and aspirations, or are they relics of a bygone era? Next, we'll explore how developing the right metrics can not only gauge but also enhance the very culture we strive to cultivate. It's not just about measuring success—it's about defining it.

CHAPTER 20:
RETHINKING SAFETY METRICS

"If the metrics you are looking at aren't useful in optimizing your strategy - stop looking at them."
– Mark Twain

In our quest for a safer workplace, it is essential to focus on meaningful metrics—those that truly reflect and drive safety improvements, align with cultural goals, and inspire a genuine commitment to safety beyond compliance.

In a busy metal fabrication facility, safety signs adorned every wall, and reports boasted zero injuries. Yet beneath the surface, near misses went unreported, and minor injuries climbed. The focus on Total Recordable Incident Rate (TRIR) created a false sense of security. Only after a serious forklift accident did leadership realize the flaw: the numbers looked good, but the culture was quietly deteriorating.

Management was befuddled. How could their prized metric—the one they believed defined their safety mindset—be misleading? The answer was uncomfortably simple: the injury rate was painting a skewed picture. By focusing solely on this rate, the company was unintentionally discouraging the reporting of minor incidents and near misses, driving workers to prioritize speed over caution just to fit the metrics.

This journey teaches us an invaluable lesson: our metrics not only measure performance but also shape behavior. When companies focus on numbers that no longer reflect the true state of safety, they jeopardize the very safety they seek to guarantee. As workplaces evolve, so must our approach to measuring safety to foster an environment where actual safety improvements take precedence over just trying to meet regulatory requirements.

It's tempting to assume that legacy safety metrics like Days Away Restriction and Transfer (DART) or Total Recordable Incident Rate (TRIR) suffice in assessing workplace safety. These numbers produce neat, quantifiable assessments, allowing companies to publicly tout safety victories. Yet these traditional metrics represent a superficial glance into a vast, hidden expanse.

Traditional metrics are often a double-edged sword. By focusing narrowly on lost time incidents or recordable cases, companies inadvertently prioritize quantity over quality. The simplicity of these metrics reduces complex safety dynamics to pure numbers, often ignoring the underlying causes or context of incidents. They can create a misleading picture where fewer recorded injuries might denote either improved safety or, more troublingly, lower incident reporting due to fear of repercussions or complex paperwork.

Metrics like TRIR are fundamentally reactive—calculating injuries after they happen. This backward-facing outlook fosters a mindset of response rather than prevention. It cues companies to brace for impact rather than proactively anticipate and circumvent safety issues. For instance, if an incident doesn't result in a lost day, it might not be captured, although the near miss could signify a severe risk looming ahead.

Companies entrapped by traditional metrics often exhibit a form of "number-blindness." They may celebrate when statistics hint at safety improvements, oblivious to the echoes of underlying peril. It's essential to recognize when metrics become ends rather than means, distorting incentives. Workers focus on avoiding recordable incidents to present a prettier picture for managerial dashboards rather than addressing the root concerns impacting their safety daily.

In essence, conventional safety metrics, by design, prioritize the quantitative tally of incidents over qualitative analysis, limiting their utility in truly enhancing workplace safety. By digging beneath these surface-level numbers, organizations can begin to redesign how they measure—and thus improve—workplace safety.

The 2005 BP Texas City Refinery explosion serves as a tragic example of how low injury rates can mask catastrophic risk. Despite boasting stellar TRIR scores, the plant was riddled with neglected safety systems and cultural blind spots. On March 23, an explosion killed 15 and injured over 170. The disaster wasn't a failure of metrics—it was a failure of meaning. BP's focus on compliance and numbers had blinded leadership to deeper, systemic risks.

The underlying safety ethos was obscured by a focus on quantifiable injury data, which neglected the precarious conditions created by inadequate safety systems and a disregard for potentially catastrophic risks.

On the day of the BP explosion, I was attending a Process Hazard Analysis (PHA) meeting, discussing the controls we had implemented to minimize the risk of a similar event at a chemical plant in Texas. Being in a room with colleagues focused on reducing explosion risks, only to later hear about the Texas City explosion, was jarring—a profound moment for our

PHA team. We dug deeper into our systems to ensure we had robust controls in place.

Investigations later uncovered a troubling pattern: cost-cutting measures had resulted in outdated equipment and poorly executed safety protocols. Alarmingly, a report by the U.S. Chemical Safety and Hazard Investigation Board (CSB) indicated that many of these issues were longstanding and had been reported but ignored.

In essence, BP's management was misled by the illusion of safety efficacy produced by impressive injury rate statistics, while insufficient attention was paid to process safety management and overall culture. BP had fallen into the trap of prioritizing "compliance over people," focusing heavily on adherence to minimum standards and metrics rather than fostering an environment that encouraged genuine dialogue and vigilance regarding safety risks.

The post-accident investigations prompted extensive reflection and critique of BP's reliance on injury rates as the primary safety measure. Safety audits and incident logs were overlooked in favor of statistical achievements. Unfortunately, this led to a false sense of security—a belief that the refinery was safer than it truly was, perpetuated by a culture that failed to embrace holistic safety principles.

The Texas City incident revealed a sobering truth: low injury rates and regulatory compliance do not guarantee a safe working environment. True safety leadership requires an ingrained commitment to safety, where every employee feels responsible for both their own safety and that of their colleagues and the entire industrial ecosystem. Leadership must strive to go beyond basic compliance, creating an environment where safety becomes a deeply rooted cultural value.

The aftermath of the explosion was transformative for BP. With legal penalties mounting and its reputation damaged, the company committed to revitalizing its safety initiatives. John Browne, BP's Group Chief Executive at the time, openly acknowledged the need for dramatic changes in safety protocols and management structure. While the transition took years, BP began to integrate process safety management more thoroughly into its operations, emphasizing the importance of addressing systemic risks rather than focusing solely on injury numbers.

This painful reckoning at BP underscores a universal truth: outdated metrics can blind leaders to real risks. Their story serves as a powerful reminder of why evolving our measurement tools is not just smart—it's essential for saving lives. It highlights the need for companies to cultivate environments where safety transcends metrics, becoming an intrinsic organizational value.

Leaders must drive this transformation by promoting transparency, learning from past events, and striving for continuous improvement. Ultimately, a positive safety model anticipates danger, communicates effectively, and prioritizes the well-being of every stakeholder involved.

In the pursuit of a safer workplace, striving to only meet compliance with outdated safety metrics is insufficient. Forward-thinking companies are adopting innovative methods that better capture the complexities of safety dynamics. Here are some approaches organizations can leverage to modernize safety measurement:

- **Leading Indicators:** Track proactive behaviors (e.g., training hours, audit frequency) to prevent incidents before they occur.
- **Behavior-Based Observations:** Encourage real-time reinforcement of safe practices through peer feedback.

- **Safety Climate Surveys:** Measure employee perceptions to uncover cultural misalignments.
- **Near-Miss Reporting Systems:** Capture and analyze potential hazards before they result in harm.
- **Smart Technology:** Utilize IoT devices and wearables for real-time data and alerts.
- **Integrated Safety Management Systems (ISMS):** Align safety metrics with broader organizational processes and goals. For instance, a manufacturing firm might integrate safety data with production dashboards, tracking both output and leading safety indicators side by side. This integration helps leaders make decisions with full visibility of operational and safety trade-offs.

By transitioning to these innovative safety measurement approaches, organizations enhance their understanding of safety effectiveness and cultivate a proactive culture that is deeply integrated with their operational goals.

You might be asking yourself, "How do metrics influence culture?"

Consider how you measure quality in your products. Can we apply the same rigor to safety? If a faulty product doesn't meet standards, should we view an injury during production as a similar red flag? Is it truly a good product if someone was hurt making it? Perhaps we should all be using metrics like these to genuinely measure success.

In the realm of workplace safety, metrics are more than numbers; they are powerful determinants that shape the culture of an organization. These measurements do more than track performance—they set the tone, define expectations, and influence behaviors across all levels of the company.

Metrics shape not just performance, but behavior. When companies prioritize TRIR or DART, they may unintentionally reward underreporting or risk-avoidance. By shifting to proactive metrics—like near-miss tracking, audit participation, or safety feedback—leaders convey a clear message: safety isn't about numbers; it's about values and vigilance.

Effective metrics also foster transparency and accountability. By regularly reviewing and openly discussing safety metrics, organizations create an environment where safety is a shared responsibility. Employees at all levels become involved in safety discussions, contributing to a more open dialogue about enhancing safety practices. This inclusiveness can boost morale and foster a deep-seated sense of accountability toward individual and collective safety goals.

By adopting innovative safety metrics that provide meaningful insights and foster employee engagement, companies encourage creative problem-solving and innovation. Metrics that emphasize learning and improvement, such as those tracking training efficacy or audit comprehensiveness, stimulate employees to adopt safer, more effective practices and suggest enhancements. This forward-thinking approach can dynamically evolve safety initiatives within the organization.

Metrics drive behavior—and culture. When companies reward low injury rates without context, they may unintentionally suppress reporting. Conversely, tracking proactive behaviors like audits and peer observations signals that prevention and participation are valued more than appearances. What we choose to measure communicates to our people what we truly value.

Metrics can be powerful trust builders—when used transparently and fairly. Sharing safety data openly helps employees feel respected and included, while basing decisions on clear metrics reduces bias and fosters accountability. When teams are empowered with data, they feel more confident in contributing to improvements. Used effectively, metrics become more than tools—they evolve into a language of trust.

Metrics provide a level playing field where performance and safety practices are judged based on clear, objective data rather than subjective opinions. This fairness in evaluation helps reduce bias, holds both leaders and employees accountable, and reassures team members that their efforts are recognized based on merit.

Providing employees access to safety data empowers them to participate actively in safety initiatives. When teams can see and analyze data themselves, they feel better equipped to suggest improvements and make informed decisions.

By consistently using metrics as a communication tool, leaders reinforce key safety messages and priorities. Regular updates and reviews of safety metrics help maintain a steady dialogue about safety, ensuring that employees understand how their work contributes to broader safety goals.

When leaders actively reference metrics to guide decisions, they visibly demonstrate their commitment to safety and improvement. This data-driven approach shows employees that decisions are based on facts rather than whims, underscoring leaders' dedication to creating a safer work environment.

Well-chosen and transparently used metrics can enhance trust by promoting fairness, transparency, and accountability, while empowering employees with data and reinforcing a consistent safety narrative.

Metrics shape not only performance but also behavior. When companies prioritize TRIR or DART, they may inadvertently reward underreporting or risk-avoidance. By shifting to proactive metrics—such as near-miss tracking, audit participation, or safety feedback—leaders convey a clear message: safety is about principles, values, and vigilance, not just numbers.

When our metrics reflect our values—promoting transparency, prevention, and shared responsibility—they do more than track safety; they help build it. This is how we transform numbers into an intentional culture and accountability into trust.

BONUS INSIGHTS

I would like to share some insights based on my lived experience and what I've learned from trusted leaders. We must continue learning from one another and remember that people must come before profits. It's not just about policies—it's about how we care for each other. Safety begins with every decision, at every level. Here are some thoughts to consider for different scenarios:

For Hourly Operations: You are on the front lines, facing risks directly, unlike those behind desks. Always assess risks and avoid shortcuts. If something doesn't feel safe or a procedure seems off, speak up. Your voice could save lives.

For Maintenance and Construction Teams: You're in the thick of it too. While you may have fewer guidelines, your ability to evaluate risks and communicate is crucial. Stop, think, and ask before diving into a task. It may slow things down initially, but it prevents accidents and keeps everyone safe.

For Supervisors: You hold one of the most influential roles. Prioritize people over production. Continuously improve safety procedures, ensure your team goes home safe, and get to know your employees. Staying attentive can help you notice when someone is having a tough day.

For Engineers: Your work, often seen as solitary, is vital for fostering a collaborative atmosphere. Early collaboration with operational staff can greatly improve outcomes, reduce costs, and build trust. Value every team member's insights to drive safety from the ground up.

For Managers: Like supervisors, your actions set the tone. Walk the walk—address issues as they arise. Continuously ask whether a situation could lead to injury, rather than just checking if it meets standards.

For Safety Professionals: Our roles have evolved! We are beyond compliance now. Engage employees in discussions that lead to innovative solutions. Coaching rather than lecturing makes a significant difference in helping teams internalize safety practices.

For Executives: You are steering the change across industries. Keep communication lines open and encourage input from all levels. Don't overlook insights and suggestions that could make a significant difference.

For Families Who've Suffered Loss: Please continue to share your stories. Your voices are essential for shaping safer workplace environments. We are committed to ensuring that people always come first in safety considerations.

Let's make safety more than a requirement—let's make it our way of life. Together, we can create a safer, more supportive workplace for everyone.

EPILOGUE

Dear Readers,

As we conclude this book, I want to reflect on why this journey into safety is not just a professional endeavor but a deeply personal one. My aim in writing this book was to transcend the notion of safety as an occupational obligation and inspire leaders at all levels to view safety as an opportunity to make profound, lasting impacts on lives and communities. This journey is more than a professional path—it's deeply personal. I still remember standing beside a grieving family after a preventable incident. That moment etched a conviction in me: safety leadership must be about people, not just paperwork and posters.

Safety is not merely a career path; it's a calling that resonates with my personal convictions. Chapter 2 offered a glimpse into this passion. The story that began this book is the same one that concludes it—a call to lead with intention, not obligation. While the lessons may have deepened, the purpose remains: to protect what matters most. It's not about adhering to regulations because we must, but because every preventive action could mean a life saved, a family kept whole, and a community safeguarded.

A recurring theme in this journey has been challenging leaders to redefine safety—not just to meet regulations but to reimagine what's possible when safety becomes a living, breathing part of organizational identity.

I urge every reader to embrace safety as a cornerstone of leadership. This approach fosters environments where people feel both protected and empowered to lead, speak up, and shape their surroundings.

The narratives and strategies outlined in Chapter 1 and the subsequent chapters highlight the necessity of weaving safety into the fabric of responsibility and care—not as an afterthought but as a priority.

Let us recognize that safety is, at its core, an expression of care and responsibility. Its true measure isn't solely in the metrics of lost-time injuries but in the peace of mind it brings to everyone involved. As you continue in your roles, remember this: compliance forms the foundation upon which you can build a fortress of safety, innovation, and trust.

So, here's your invitation: be the leader who raises the bar. Don't settle for minimum standards—elevate them. Empower your teams, question outdated metrics, and lead with courage, trust, and commitment. Together, we can create workplaces that don't just comply with safety— they embody it.

Warm regards,

Mickey Hannum

ACKNOWLEDGEMENTS

To my loving wife and family, thank you for your endless encouragement and support, pushing me to finish what I started numerous times. Your belief in me kept the momentum alive, and this book exists today because you convinced me to keep going.

I extend my deepest gratitude to all the remarkable individuals I've learned from over the years. Whether you were a leader who shaped my beliefs or a colleague on the swing shift production floor who shared the challenges of working with limited sleep, you have all profoundly impacted my journey.

Acknowledgement also goes to process safety directors, production managers, plant managers, engineers, and safety professionals—your insights and dedication have made it easy for me to learn from you. My career, both in the USA and internationally, has been a continuous learning opportunity, thanks to all of you. I will always be a lifelong learner—made even more inspired, curious, and driven by everything you've shared with me.

I would also like to extend my heartfelt gratitude to Jeet Radia and Michelle Berardinelli for their invaluable feedback on this project. Your insights and support have been truly instrumental, helping me refine my ideas and clarify the message I want readers to take away from this book. I deeply appreciate your contributions.

Finally, to everyone reading this book, I hope you find at least one thing within these pages that aids you in your journey. Together, through shared knowledge and experiences, the challenges of making workplaces safer become easier to overcome. Remember, we are not alone in this mission to create environments where everyone feels valued.

Thank you for being part of this path toward safer workplaces.

REFERENCES

Chapter 2

- Bureau of Labor Statistics. "Employer-Reported Workplace Injuries and Illnesses-2021." *U.S. Department of Labor*, https://www.bls.gov/iif/. Accessed 2023.
- International Labour Organization. "Safety and health at the heart of the future of work: Building on 100 years of experience." *ILO*, https://www.ilo.org/global/publications. Accessed 2023.
- Liberty Mutual Workplace Safety Index. "The ROI of Workplace Safety." *Liberty Mutual*, 2022.
- Mine Safety and Health Administration. "Upper Big Branch Mine-South, Report of Investigation." *U.S. Department of Labor*, www.msha.gov/upper-big-branch-mine-south-april-5-2010.
- National Safety Council. "The Cost of Workplace Injuries." *National Safety Council*, 2021.
- New Zealand Government. "Pike River Recovery Agency." *New Zealand Government*, pikeriverrecovery.govt.nz.
- New Zealand Government. "Royal Commission on the Pike River Coal Mine Tragedy." *New Zealand Government*, 2012. pikeriver.royalcommission.govt.nz.
- NPR. "Timeline: West Virginia's Upper Big Branch mine disaster." *NPR*, www.npr.org/sections/thetwo-way/2011/06/29/137479038.
- Occupational Safety and Health Administration. "Workers' Compensation Costs." *OSHA*, 2021.

- PBS. "The Spill: Who's accountable for the deadliest U.S. mining disaster?" *PBS*, www.pbs.org/wgbh/pages/frontline/the-spill/.

Chapter 3

- Bailey, Sarah. "Five Ways BP Transformed Its Safety Culture." *Forbes*, 2015.
- Energy Institute. "Hearts and Minds." *Energy Institute*, www.energyinst.org/programme/hearts-and-minds.
- Gallup. "State of the American Workplace." *Gallup*, 2017.
- Gallup. "What Is Employee Engagement and How Do You Improve It?" *Gallup.com*, 2023.
- Geller, E. Scott. "Behavior-Based Safety and Occupational Risk Management." *Behavior and Social Issues*, 2014.
- Harvard Business Review. "After the Spill: Transforming Safety Leadership at BP." *Harvard Business Review*.
- Johnson, Rob.
- Liker, Jeffrey K. *The Toyota Way: 14 Management Principles from the World's Greatest Manufacturer.* McGraw-Hill, 2004.
- Roswell, John M., et al. "Engagement and Performance: A Meta-Analysis." *University of Michigan Studies in Organizational Behavior*, 2019.
- Shell. "Our Focus on Safety." *Shell Global*, www.shell.com/sustainability/safety/our-focus-on-safety.html.
- Shell Global. "Energy and Innovation: Safety." *Shell*, https://www.shell.com/energy-and-innovation/safety.html. Accessed October 10, 2023.
- "Does Toyota's Culture Explain Its Quality Problems?" *Harvard Business Review*, 2010. https://hbr.org.

- "Employee Engagement and Safety: A Connection." *Journal of Occupational and Environmental Medicine*, 2017.

Chapter 4
- Covey, Stephen M.R. *The Speed of Trust: The One Thing That Changes Everything.* Free Press, 2006.
- Duhigg, Charles. *The Power of Habit: Why We Do What We Do in Life and Business.* Random House, 2012.
- Fortune. "Building Safer Workplaces: Alcoa's Journey." *Fortune.*
- Harvard Business Review. "Building a Safety Culture." *Harvard Business Review.*
- O'Neill, Paul. "Interview on Leadership and Safety."

Chapter 5
- Edmondson, Amy C. *The Fearless Organization: Creating Psychological Safety in the Workplace for Learning, Innovation, and Growth.* Wiley, 2019.
- Harvard Business School. "Edmondson, Amy C." *Harvard Business School.* Accessed 2023.

Chapter 6
- Quality Assurance Journal. "The Five Whys: A Tool for Continuous Improvement." *Quality Assurance Journal*, 2023.
- Safety Institute. "Root Cause Analysis: A Safety Management System Technique." *Safety Management Guide*, 2022.
- Senge, Peter M. *The Fifth Discipline: The Art & Practice of the Learning Organization.* Doubleday/Currency, 2006.

Chapter 7

- DuPont. "About Safety." *DuPont*, www.dupont.com/about/safety.html.
- Geller, E. Scott. "Safety in Numbers." *Harvard Business Review*, 2005. hbr.org/2005/11/safety-in-numbers.

Chapter 8

- Edwards, B., & Baker, A. (2020). Bob's Guide to Operational Learning: How to Think Like a Human and Organizational Performance (HOP) Coach.
- Lee, H. (1960). To Kill a Mockingbird. J.B. Lippincott & Co.

Chapter 9

- Hannum, M. (2025, February 5). Change your culture. Change your safety. Modern Casting.

Chapter 10

- Cahill, Lawrence B. *Environmental Health and Safety Audits: A Compendium of Thoughts and Trends.* CRC Press, 2007.

Chapter 11

- Business Insider. "The Former CEO of Alcoa Changed the Company's Entire Culture by Focusing on One Key Area." *Business Insider*.
- Crichton, Michael. *Jurassic Park.* Ballantine Books, 1990.
- Duhigg, Charles. *The Power of Habit: Why We Do What We Do in Life and Business.* Random House, 2012.
- Harvard Business Review. "How Paul O'Neill Made Alcoa Healthier and More Profitable." *Harvard Business Review*.

- Spielberg, Steven, director. *Jurassic Park.* Universal Pictures, 1993.

Chapter 12
- Reuters. "Siemens Shifts Focus to a 'Zero Harm Culture'." *Reuters*, www.reuters.com/article/us-siemens-safety-focus-idUSKBN1ZH0ZY.
- Siemens. "Health & Safety." *Siemens*, new.siemens.com/global/en/company/sustainability/health-and-safety.html.

Chapter 13
- ConocoPhillips. "Safety and Sustainability Report." *ConocoPhillips*, 2020.
- Cummins Inc. "Sustainability Report." *Cummins Inc.*, 2021.
- Dekker, Sidney. *Safety Differently: Human Factors for a New Era.* Ashgate Publishing, 2014.
- Geller, E. Scott. "Ten Principles of Behavior-Based Safety." *Professional Safety*, 2002.
- Intermountain Healthcare. "Clinical Program Leadership and Performance Improvement." *Institute for Healthcare Improvement.*
- Smith, Devon. "Applying BBS in a High-Risk Industry." *International Journal of Occupational Safety and Ergonomics*, 2021.
- Smith, John. "Transforming Healthcare with Trust: A Study of Intermountain Healthcare." *Harvard Business Review*, 2017.
- WestRock Company. *WestRock*, www.westrock.com. Accessed April 28, 2025.

Chapter 14

- Agency for Healthcare Research and Quality. "Notes from the Field: Just Culture." *Agency for Healthcare Research and Quality*, 2017. www.ahrq.gov/patient-safety/reports/engage/notes4.html.
- Harvard Business Review. "Rethinking Hierarchy in Organizations." *Harvard Business Review*, 2011.
- Marx, David. "Just Culture: Balancing Safety and Accountability." *By Your Side: Patient Safety and Quality Improvement*, American Nurses Association, 2001.
- Morgan, Jacob. *The Future of Work: Attract New Talent, Build Better Leaders, and Create a Competitive Organization.* Wiley, 2014.
- Sherwood, Gwen, and Jane Barnsteiner. "Patient Safety and Quality: Page 1." *Evidence-Based Handbook for Nurses*, Agency for Healthcare Research and Quality, 2008.

Chapter 15

- Hoffman, Reid, Chris Yeh, and Satya Nadella. *Blitzscaling.* Crown, 2018.
- Kirkland, Rik. "Microsoft CEO Satya Nadella: Transforming Culture and Capabilities to Change the Game..." *McKinsey & Company*, 2019.
- Nadella, Satya. *Hit Refresh: The Quest to Rediscover Microsoft's Soul...* Harper Business, 2017.

Chapter 16

- Energy Industry Leadership Conference. "Energy Industry Leadership Conference Reports." 2006.

- International Journal of Industrial Ergonomics. "Integrating Leadership and Safety Practices in Industrial Settings." *International Journal of Industrial Ergonomics*, 2008.
- Shell. "Frontline Leadership Development at Shell." *Shell Company Press Releases*, 2005.

Chapter 17

- Alaska Airlines. "Safety Innovations." *Alaska Airlines*, https://www.alaskaair.com/. Accessed October 2024.

Chapter 18

- Business Strategy Review. "The Evolution of DuPont's Industrial Safety Culture." *Business Strategy Review*, 2021.
- DuPont. "DuPont Sustainable Solutions." *DuPont*, www.dupont.com/about/dupont-sustainable-solutions.html.
- Gulati, Ravi. "The Evolution of DuPont's Industrial Safety Culture." *Business Strategy Review*, 2021.
- Industrial Safety Journals. "Safety Leadership: DuPont's Legacy." *Industrial Safety Journals*, 2020.
- Liker, Jeffrey K. *The Toyota Way*. McGraw-Hill, 2004.
- Toyota Global. "Toyota Production System." *Toyota Global*, www.toyota-global.com/company/vision_philosophy/toyota_production_system.
- Womack, James P., et al. *The Machine That Changed the World*. Free Press, 1990.

Chapter 19

- Taylor, F. W. (1911). The Principles of Scientific Management. Harper & Brothers
- Wilms, W. W., Hardcastle, A. J., & Zell, D. M. (1994). Cultural Transformation at NUMMI. MIT Sloan Management Review.

Chapter 20

- Broadribb, M. P. (2006). Lessons from Texas City: A Case History. Institution of Chemical Engineers.

ABOUT THE AUTHOR

Mickey Hannum is a transformative voice in business literature, known for crafting insightful, purpose-driven books that bridge leadership, safety, and cultural change. With decades of experience in safety leadership and organizational transformation, Mickey empowers leaders to create workplaces where people thrive—and return home safely every day.

His writing journey took an unexpected and heartfelt turn following a profound personal loss. A vivid dream during that time inspired him to write a children's book about trust—completed even before his first business book. This genre-crossing debut reflects Mickey's unique ability to weave meaningful storytelling into both professional and personal realms.

Born three months prematurely and given little chance of survival, Mickey's life began with a fight—and that spirit of resilience continues to define him. His early battle fuels his deep empathy, insatiable curiosity, and unwavering commitment to helping others grow, lead, and live fully.

Mickey continues to explore themes of leadership, personal growth, and transformation through his writing and speaking. Whether guiding executives or connecting with children through storytelling, his mission remains the same: to inspire courage, build trust, and champion the human spirit.